RICHARD HOUGH
BATTLESHIP

First published in the United Kingdom in 1979 by J. M. Dent & Sons Ltd as
Man O' War

This edition published in the United Kingdom in 2022 by

Canelo

Unit 9, 5th Floor

Cargo Works, 1–2 Hatfields

London, SE1 9PG

United Kingdom

A CIP catalogue record for this book is available from the British Library.

Print ISBN 978 1 80032 538 8

Ebook ISBN 978 1 80032 537 1

Look for more great books at www.canelo.co

Printed and bound in Great Britain by Clays Ltd, Elcograf S.p.A.

I

Introduction

Many authorities in 1945 believed that the era of the man o'war, as we have known her for 500 years, ceased with the dropping of atomic bombs on Japan. More than 30 years later, the deep concern with the rise of Russian naval power, from a poorly regarded and diminutive force, to the ever-growing strength it flaunts today, proves that the importance of the fighting ship is at least as great as it has ever been. Men o'war are being built, counted, assessed and exercised, their bases modernized and created, tactical and strategic considerations debated, with the same vigour today as at the beginning of the century and during the Napoleonic wars.

As I write, a war is being fought in Africa which may decide whether or not the Russian Empire will control the sea routes from the Middle East oilfields. Gunboat diplomacy is still with us; doubtless always will be. Today the theoretical debate of aircraft carrier versus nuclear submarine is as powerfully argued as battleship versus submarine from, say, 1910 until 1940. As far as the man o'war is concerned, never has the old aphorism *Plus ça change, plus c'est la même chose* applied more truly.

In this book, however, I am not concerned with the present-day fighting ship. I leave it to future historians to write of 40,000-ton amphibious assault ships, radar picket assault ships and cruiser helicopter carriers; pausing only to comment that we are in the throes of another hideous era of naval architecture. What I have attempted to provide in this book is an abbreviated history of the man o'war and her battles over 400 years by singling out chronologically examples that I consider significant and interesting, stitching them into a pattern of progress from galleon to super-Dreadnought.

In the last chapter I mention my love affair with the battleship. It began when I was a boy, and its ardour was inflamed by the Coronation Naval Review of 1937, the last occasion when the big gun platform – the battleship – was everywhere recognized as the prime weapon and arbiter in sea warfare. The marriage was consummated when I watched battleships from above going about their affairs majestically and purposefully during the 1939–45 war. Our golden wedding, so to speak, was celebrated when I took a small part in the reactivation of the mighty USS *New Jersey* in 1967, whose subsequent successful if brief career seemed to prove that the battleship was not dead after all.

I have known naval officers who have commanded diminutive motor torpedo boats, cruisers, carriers, squadrons and fleets. Whatever their varying qualities may have been, affection for their men o'war has always been a common characteristic. Lord Howard of Effingham's words of admiration for his *Ark Royal* formed themselves into an Elizabethan love ode: 'I think her the odd ship in the world for all conditions, and truly I think there can be no great ship make me change and go out of her.' Then he made sail and thrashed the Spanish Armada to prove that love and the will to win are indivisible, too.

The careers of several of the ships I have singled out were as brief as they were glorious. Both the *Bismarck* of 1941 and the *Bonhomme Richard* of 1799 succumbed after defeating their adversary in their first fight on their first operational voyage. By contrast, the Dutch *Zeven Provincien*, for example, saw de Ruyter through all his greatest battles. The *Warspite* fought through two wars, the *New Jersey* in three. The *Kelly's*, career was crowded into hectic months, the *Victory* is still a flagship after 200 years.

Richard Hough
March 1978

Acknowledgments

I am especially grateful to Admiral of the Fleet the Earl Mountbatten of Burma KG, PC, GCB, OM, etc., to the late Oliver Warner, and to Tom Pocock, for their own special contributions to this book.

R. H.

Ark Royal

Galleon, 1587, England

Accounting for the defeat of the Spanish Armada in 1588 Sir Walter Raleigh wrote:

> The Spaniard had an army aboard them, and [the English C.-in-C.] had none: they had more ships than he had of higher building and charging; so that, had he entangled himself with those great and powerful vessels, he had greatly endangered this Kingdome of England…

Raleigh himself was out of favour with Queen Elizabeth I and had a shore appointment at the time of the 'Enterprize of England', as the Spaniards called their Armada operations, but his ship, the *Ark Royal*, took a leading part in the fighting and was the flagship of Lord Howard of Effingham. In her design and construction, and in her career, there can be seen all that made English fighting ships and fighting tactics the best in the world in the sixteenth century.

For 100 years and more before the Spanish attack on England the Portuguese and Spaniards had led the world in exploration and had dominated distant maritime trading. Navigators of peerless courage had touched and charted much of the coastline of the Americas, created an empire in Central and South America, set up trading stations in Africa and India, doubled the Cape of Good Hope as well as the Horn, grown rich on the spices of the East as well as the gold of Peru.

By the Bull of Demarcation of 1493 the world – no less – had been divided into two between these Iberian powers: everyone else would, from then on, be trespassing. For these staggering accomplishments the Portuguese and Spanish sailors and traders relied largely upon caravels and carracks of the most basic design and with an overall length of no more than 100 feet.

But, as the Americans discovered 250 years later, you cannot create a merchant fleet without providing for its protection. From this need originated the Spanish and Portuguese fighting galleons, originally no more than caravels with a couple of built-up wooden castles for soldiers – a fore and an after castle. Enemy ships were not destroyed. They were captured by boarding at the waist between the castles, while the defenders hurled missiles upon them from the castles or descended to fight hand to hand with the boarders.

Defensive and offensive methods were elaborated, nets were laid in the waist to entrap the boarders, like barbed wire in the First World War. Guns were set up in the castles, and light railing pieces of doubtful reliability, but of undoubted morale-damaging usefulness, were added. Then some unknown soldier seized upon the idea of placing larger cannon in the waist itself, one or two to each side to strike at the enemy before he could board. A good solid plank was disposed above the guns to protect the crews, and acquired the name 'gunwale'. The answer to this was a second tier of guns in the waist disposed one above the other and decked over. Decks were similarly added to the castles. In this way, spasmodically over the years, there emerged the decked fighting ship with tiers of guns disposed within gun ports: the 'stately Spanish galleon'.

Henceforward the gun would be the primary weapon of sea warfare until the arrival of the super-torpedo and the bomb of the Second World War, and then the missile. But the Spanish and Portuguese, who dominated the high seas, still regarded sea fighting as an extension of land warfare and fought accordingly – soldier against soldier, the target the enemy's castles, or ship, as if the sea were no more than an inconvenient moat. Guns were for destroying the enemy's rigging, and thus his mobility.

Right up to the arrival of the steam and steel navy the Catholic nations tended to aim their guns at the enemy's rigging at 'the top of the roll', prior to coming alongside, grappling and boarding. With the coming of the gun, however, northern naval powers made sea warfare into a different art altogether. They saw the cannon as a ship-destroying weapon, firing at a relatively greater range and at the enemy's hull 'on the downward roll'.

The northern nations went for faster, nippier ships that could outmanoeuvre the enemy, raking him out of the range of his guns. Raleigh, one of the most advanced thinkers of his day as well as a man of action, claimed that 'a fleet of twenty ships, all good sailors and good ships, have the advantage, on the open sea, of an hundred as good ships, and of slower sailing'. (As proof of the unchanging nature of sea warfare, the same statement might have been made by advocates of the battle cruiser in the early twentieth century.) Raleigh continues, in his *Art of War at Sea*, to use the experience of the *Ark Royal* and her consorts at the Armada engagement to lay down a basic scheme of tactics, the twenty ships 'charging them upon any angle, shall force them to give ground, and to fall back upon their own next fellows; of which so many as entangle, are made unserviceable, or lost... after they have given one broadside of artillery, by clapping them into the wind, and staying, they may give them the other, and so the twenty ships batter them in pieces'.

Throughout the whole period of sailing ship warfare English and Swedish guns were superior in range and power to those of the Latin countries. A Spanish commander who could boast of his English guns, captured or more likely purchased through some shady dealer, was regarded with envy.

It is against this historical context that the first of the famous English *Ark Royals* can be studied. In the sixteenth century England became a considerable naval power, like France and later Holland, challenging the might of Spain and Portugal in their monopolistic trading in Africa, the Americas and the East. The circumnavigation of the world by Sir Francis Drake in 1577–80 was more than a spectacular adventure and navigational achievement. Like the captured Spanish riches he brought home, this voyage was symbolic of a new order in the unremitting struggle for power between Spain and England.

Drake's *Golden Hind* was a typical product of English construction of Elizabeth's golden age. We know more about ship design at this time than any earlier age because drawings and specifications giving the dimensions, configuration and rig have survived. The drawings of master shipwright Matthew Baker can be trusted. They show the *Ark Royal* and her supporting galleons at the Armada engagements as low and elegant for their time with a long single-deck forecastle, a mere vestigial castle, and with three decks aft – quarterdeck, halfdeck and poop – but again rising a comparatively small height above the waist. There is a long beakhead supported by a knee with a fine figurehead at the extremity. The rig is simple and efficient with a very large mainsail and lower topsail and a large lateen-rigged mizzen.

Contemporary paintings are less trustworthy. Like commissioned drawings of country houses or nineteenth-century racehorses, these were often done to flatter their owners, and contemporary taste did not always accord with efficient practice. It seems likely that a multiplicity of topsails and high forecastles and poop decks were considered fashionably *de rigueur* long after the shipwright and fighting sailor knew better. Probably the fanciful and elaborate galleons with billowing flags and streamers that hung proudly on the walls of country mansions bore little relation to the sharp, swift, comparatively low-profile fighting ships of that time. If the rig was as elaborate as depicted, the practical sailor no doubt dealt properly with it when at sea, just as hardened sea dogs would order their carpenter to hack off heavy and elaborate carving fitted by the show-off owner.

In 1586 Sir Walter Raleigh ordered from Mr R. Chapman of Deptford on the Thames, an armed vessel of some 700 tons for his colonial activities in

Virginia. She was to be named the *Ark*, followed by his own name as a suffix in accordance with custom. The *Ark* was launched on 12 June 1587.

The only contemporary picture of her is unfortunately in the usual florid and caricatured style. But no doubt the basic characteristics are correct, with two gundecks, the excellent long-ranging culverins and demi-culverins behind lids when not in use, four masts – fore, main, mizzen and bonaventure mizzen – the last two lateen rigged, and a veritable extravaganza of streamers, flags and bunting. The decoration and carving is also depicted as elaborate, and at the square-cut stern above the four guns on two decks there is a gallery.

The prominent beakhead to protect the bows in heavy seas supports a long bowsprit. The quality of the *Ark Raleigh* and her kind lay in their ability to manoeuvre swiftly, fire port and starboard broadsides as Raleigh advocated, keeping all the time well beyond the range of their opponents' shorter ranging guns.

Even before she was fitted out at Deptford, the increasingly threatening intentions of Spain were clear, and the country was preparing for invasion by the combined forces of an Armada from

Lisbon and the Duke of Parma's forces from the Low Countries. Raleigh therefore sold his fine new ship to the Queen. No money actually changed hands; instead, and characteristically, Queen Elizabeth reduced Raleigh's debt to the crown by £5,000. The great ship was then renamed *Ark Royal* although she was customarily referred to as the *Arke*.

She was at once selected by the Lord High Admiral, Lord Charles Howard, as his flagship. He appreciated her qualities, writing to Lord Burghley, the Queen's chief secretary of state, of her sailing qualities, 'We can see no sail, great nor small, but how far soever they be off, we fetch them and speak with them.' To Sir Francis Walsingham he wrote with equal extravagance, 'I protest it before God that were it not for Her Majesty's presence I had rather live in the company of these noble ships than in any place.'

There is no doubt that the English commanders were pleased with their ships and proud of them. Sir William Wynter wrote from the *Vanguard*, 'Our ships do show themselves like gallants here. I assure you, it will do a man's heart good to behold them.'

They were less pleased with the Queen's usual parsimony in allowing ship's powder for little more than a day's hard fighting. Nor were her tactical dispositions approved by her commanders. Sir Francis Drake was the most vigorous proponent of the offensive policy. As early as March 1588 he was begging to be allowed to fight the enemy off the Tagus: '…your Majesty stand assured, with God's assistance, that if the fleet come out of Lisbon, as long as we have victual to live withal upon that coast, they shall be fort with.'

With his unmatched experience of fighting the Spanish, Drake was absolutely right that if possible the Armada should 'not come through the seas as conquerors'. Instead, the Queen held back her fleet. Drake may or may not have been playing bowls when the Spanish fleet was sighted off the Lizard; and he may or may not have told those about him that the Spaniards 'must wait their turn' for his attention. What we can be sure of is that, having failed to persuade the Queen to let him take the offensive from the start, he would react calmly to the news. With a south-westerly wind blowing and the tide flooding into the sound no one could have sailed from Plymouth anyway.

And so it came about that Drake with the *Revenge* and Howard in the *Ark Royal* warped out of Plymouth Sound after the tide turned at 10 pm followed by their squadrons, and by masterly seamanship extricated themselves from the unfortunate tactical situation into which the Queen had placed them. They succeeded in getting the weather gage of the Armada by dawn, Sunday 21 July, 'decrying their fleet', reported Howard from the *Ark Royal*, 'to consist of 120 sail … many ships of great burthen. At nine o'clock we gave them fight, which continued until one.'

At this stage the English fleet was greatly outnumbered and could only pursue a policy of harassment, chivvying along the great wedge-shaped formation to discourage it from closing the English shore. But before hostilities could break out Howard and Medina Sidonia were obliged to perform the formalities in accordance with chivalric custom. The Spaniard as 'Captain-General of the Ocean Sea' hoisted his sacred banner instructing engagement, and from the *Ark Royal* Howard despatched his personal pinnace to carry his challenge to the Captain-General.

With the completion of these overtures, Howard sailed the *Ark Royal* in on the Armada's rearguard, engaging the *Rata Coronada*, a vessel of similar size and power to his own but much higher out of the water. The Spanish galleon put over her helm in an attempt to close the range, but Howard was having none of that and kept his distance, firing his culverins from beyond the range of the Spanish cannon. Meanwhile, Drake, Frobisher and Hawkins led their squadrons into a wing of the rearguard, cutting out one of the largest galleons, the *San Juan*, pounding it from a safe distance and evading all the Portuguese efforts to grapple and board.

As the morning wore on Medina Sidonia recovered his errant galleon, the *Rata Coronada* rejoined her formation, and the Armada resumed its course up-Channel, as seemingly invincible as King Philip had boasted to the world. From this early encounter it appeared that Medina Sidonia's galleons were impervious to the long-range English gunfire. For their part the Spanish and Portuguese ships were incapable of closing and boarding the enemy. A slow-moving stalemate was the result.

All the way to the Isle of Wight the *Ark Royal* and her consorts continued their harrying attacks like terriers worrying a lumbering bull, hoping to demoralize the enemy but making no significant impression with their tip-and-run broadsides. Medina Sidonia's only damage resulted from mishaps. One of his galleons collided within the tight-packed formation, fell astern, could not be recovered by a towrope in the rising seas, and was later captured by Drake. Another was crippled by a powder explosion.

The fighting flared up off Portland Bill and the Isle of Wight, where Howard feared they might attack and take possession of the island as a base. At one point a flat calm descended upon the two fleets. Again there were one or two stragglers from the Armada, and Howard ordered the *Ark Royal*'s boats out to tow the flagship to within range of them. Medina Sidonia had with him four galleasses, heavily armed vessels of a crossbreed between galleon and galley which had won for the Christian fleet the recent Battle of Lepanto against the Turkish Fleet. These were perfect galleass conditions, and he sent three of them to the rescue of the stragglers. The English at once engaged them.

'There were many good shots', boasted Howard, claiming that one was nearly sunk 'and another by a shot from the Arke lost her lantern which came swimming by, and the third his nose [ram]…'

When the wind got up again the Armada resumed its progress and slowly regained its formation while the English squadrons continued their alert, cautious shadowing. The first preoccupation of both sides was ammunition. The English, at first profligate and later more economical in the expenditure of their meagre supplies of powder and shot, were now desperately short. Medina Sidonia was little better off. Moreover the Armada could expect no additional supplies until the rendezvous with Parma. For his part Howard despatched pinnaces to land at selected points along the coast to scour stores for ammunition. Then he rejoined his fleet and, a week after that first exchange of fire, observed Medina Sidonia anchor his fleet off Calais.

There was no sign of the Duke of Parma, who in fact was far away in Bruges, quite unprepared for the Armada's arrival and with his fleet bottled in by Dutch Sea Beggars, as the rebellious Dutch were called. Howard himself, however, was further strengthened by the arrival of two squadrons which had been guarding the Thames against an attack by Parma.

It had to be accepted that so far English gunnery had failed. There had been none of Raleigh's 'battering them in pieces', and there was much depression on the English side. But now luck and ingenuity came to Howard's rescue. With wind and tide in his favour, he made preparations for a fireship attack on the massed enemy whose masts were like a forest in winter off the French coast.

The English had eight of these dreaded vessels, packed tight with inflammable material, their guns with double-headed shot. Now they were released in tight-packed formation in the dark and before the rising wind. Medina Sidonia had been warned of the danger by Philip before embarking, and when he observed the fast-moving torches approach, guns discharging under the heat, he ordered all cables cut and his fleet close-hauled out to sea.

The inevitable result was a panic-stricken shambles. One of the galleasses, its rudder damaged, was driven ashore off Calais. At dawn a single shot from the *Ark Royal* ordered the combined English fleets into battle against the disordered and scattered enemy, although Howard did not at once conform to his own order.

The crew of the flagship, like many others, had their eye on that stranded galleass. In the only misjudgment of the campaign, Howard allowed his men to 'have pillage of her'. Drake and Frobisher, Seymour and Wynter and the rest were already battering the Spanish and Portuguese ships which were fighting at a crippling disadvantage off a lee shore, before the *Ark Royal* added the weight of her broadsides to the engagement.

Demoralized and now lacking the tight defensive formation they had previously held, the Spanish and Portuguese alike began to take terrible punishment. The fight became known as the Battle of Gravelines, and well named too for it proved to be the grave of many soldiers and sailors. It was one of the most decisive naval battles in history, for nothing now could save 'the Enterprize of England'.

Just as the vagaries of the wind had brought the Armada safely to Calais, had scattered it when the fireships scudded before it towards them, so now it backed towards the south-west, releasing the Armada's ships from the trap between the treacherous offshore sandbanks and the English gunfire. Medina Sidonia with his surviving ships was driven out into the North Sea, away from any hope of making a rendezvous with the Duke of Parma, and away from any hope of invading and subjugating England.

Howard from the poop deck of the *Ark Royal* observed their flight with satisfaction, while issuing orders that they must be shadowed until they were finally proved harmless. And Drake commented, 'There was never anything pleased me better than seeing the enemy flying to the northwards.'

–

The King of Spain and his people were astonishingly phlegmatic about the failure of the Enterprize of England and the loss of half the Armada that had sailed so hopefully from the Tagus. The two countries remained as mutually hostile as ever. The English continued to raid Spanish possessions and take Spanish ships at every opportunity, while remaining alert for another invasion threat. Rumours of preparations of another Armada frequently reached Queen Elizabeth's court although they were mainly false and originated in part with Spanish wishes to wear down English nerves.

The occupation of Calais in 1598 by the Spanish army intensified the vulnerability of the island to hostile attack just as it would again when Napoleon and then Hitler gazed across that narrow strip of water from the chalk cliffs of France. It also determined the English to take counter action. In twentieth-century jargon the raid on Cadiz in 1596, the *Ark Royal*'s second great operation, might be termed a pre-emptive strike by a combined operations force. Its complete success proved what could be accomplished by good planning, resolute leadership and courage.

This was to be an Anglo-Dutch operation, and although the Dutch contribution was smaller than the English the Dutch contingent played a notable part and were content to operate for the first time in history under English orders. The English command included many of the greatest of Elizabeth's 'sea dogs'. Both Drake and Frobisher had died since the Armada battles, but Raleigh was included, commanding the *Warspite*, and Sir Robert Dudley, Lord Thomas Howard and, as joint commanders-in-chief, the Earl of Essex and the Lord High Admiral, Lord Howard of Effingham.

The Queen's favourite, Essex, had overcome her reluctance to allow him to risk his life on such a dangerous expedition by promising that he would not participate personally in the attack. Essex represented the military side of the operation as distinct from the purely naval side. Again, Howard would be flying his flag in the great *Ark Royal*, which had the same armament of 55 guns as at Gravelines.

The combined fleet of some 38 fighting ships supported by auxiliaries of all kinds, bringing the total number of vessels to 150, sailed from Plymouth 1 June 1596, with instructions 'to generally injure the naval power of Spain … to take undefended towns, especially if they should be understood to contain treasure … and [as a firm royal footnote] to preserve all booty for her majesty's disposal'.

In less than three weeks the fleet was off Cadiz, which by good fortune for the Anglo-Dutch command was taken completely by surprise. The *Ark Royal* stood off the entrance to the harbour with the other big fighting ships about her, and at dawn on 21 June the first attack developed. Like several of the other larger galleons, the *Ark Royal* drew too much water to enter the harbour, and Howard transferred to a pinnace. Both the port's batteries and some heavily-armed galleys countered with a fierce fire, resisting for a time the English attack. It was more than Essex could bear not to participate and he hurled himself into the battle at the same time as his joint commander-in-chief sailed his pinnace into the teeth of the Spanish gunfire.

Slowly and bloodily the English forced back the galleys and at length put them into confused retreat. The Spaniards began to fire their own big ships rather than let them fall into enemy hands, but two 1,200-ton galleons were saved from the holocaust by Howard's men. The Dutch contingent was meanwhile attacking Puntal successfully, and by noon Essex was at the gate of the city of Cadiz itself. His men scaled the walls, putting to flight the Spanish defence force of 500 men, and then worked through the narrow streets to complete the occupation and accept the surrender of the city.

In this Cadiz raid the Anglo-Dutch force caused Spain a loss of some 20 million ducats, including around 37 ships burned, others captured, 1,200 guns captured or destroyed, and vast quantities of loot. Howard and Essex and the Dutch commander were in favour of proceeding to the Azores to lie in wait for homeward-bound Spanish carracks but the other captains voted that enough was enough and were not prepared to risk the loss of what they had already acquired.

In spite of this savage blow to the strength and pride of Spain, King Philip continued with his plans to invade England. In the following year another Armada was prepared by the dogged but now ailing king. The Spanish seemed to have learned no lessons from the previous disaster. It was as if the Battle of Gravelines had never been fought. But this time the *Ark Royal*, manned and victualled and with a full complement of powder and shot, was not called upon to defend her nation. For the wind, which had been the final decisive factor nine years earlier, scattered and sent home the Armada before it could even reach the Channel. God, it was said, did not intend Catholic Spain to conquer the little island of infidels.

King Philip died shortly after this failure, and his undefeated adversary, Queen Elizabeth, died in 1603. Under King James I the English navy began to slide into one of its declines, in morale as well as in *matériel*. The economical new sovereign ordered the repair instead of the scrapping of his ageing flagship. She reappeared in her new guise in 1608. Even her name was changed, to *Anne Royal* after the new Queen. Her days of greatness were over. When preparations for another attack on Cadiz were made in 1625, the *Anne Royal* sailed once again as flagship, this time of Lord Wimbledon, but to disaster instead of triumph. The expedition was a fiasco, disease struck the men, and when the flagship limped back to England more than half her company were dead or sick.

Eleven years later, in 1636, the old ship was involved in an accident which suggested to some that she died of shame by her own hand. In the Medway, preparing to act as flagship once more, she stove herself on her own anchors, listed over and sank. Then, when she was raised from her shallow grave, she was found to be so rotten as not to be worth the cost of repair, and was broken up.

Three more vessels inheriting the name 'Ark Royal' have served with the Royal Navy, all of them in this century, all with special distinction, and all in the new branch of aviation. The first was the world's first aircraft carrier, completed in 1914; the second the most famous and most frequently 'sunk' (according to German propaganda) carrier of the Second World War; the third the Royal Navy's largest carrier, still afloat at the time this book went to press.

Zeven Provincien

Galleon, 1665, Holland

The Dutch, those gritty mariners and traders, thrice challenged England's arrogant claims of imperial and economic monopoly in the seventeenth century. These wars between two Protestant peoples who had, only recently, successfully defeated Catholic Spain, were as fiercely fought as any religious campaign. They were also unsatisfactory wars for both protagonists who suffered grievously for little gain.

These Dutch wars marked the coming of age of sea warfare. The naval officer became a professional instead of a part-timer lending his services and even his ship to the nation when it was threatened, before returning to the more lucrative business of trading or privateering. Fighting at sea became more formalized, with laid-down tactics.

The English even published the first tactical code book entitled 'Fighting Instructions'.

The 'line of battle', in which ships fought drawn up in opposed parallel lines instead of fighting in a mêlée, was established – thus 'line-of-battle-ship' and 'battleship'. 'Nothing equals the beautiful order of the English at sea,' wrote the Comte de Guiche, an observer with the Dutch fleet. 'Never was a line drawn straighter than that formed by their ships.'

Signalling became more elaborate, discipline more formalized. Above all, it was the end of the converted merchantman as a fighting ship. No longer did one sail into battle in a trading vessel equipped with extra guns. Navies became permanent establishments of fighting ships officered by professionals.

–

The Dutch suffered a number of handicaps as a maritime and trading nation. The first was their geographical situation. Whichever door a ship left by, the northern or the western, she had to pass close by English shores. A powerful English navy could effectively blockade the trade of these northern European states, as it later succeeded in blockading Germany in two world wars. Second, the Dutch coastline was thick with shoals and shifting sands which were a hazard to navigation and restricted the draught of her merchantmen and fighting ships alike. Then, every length of timber for the construction of her fleets had to be imported from the Baltic, which was inconvenient, expensive and politically and strategically disadvantageous. Finally, the recently united provinces – the Zeven Provincien – did not always behave in a united manner. There was jealousy and feuds with results that were sometimes disastrous in naval operations.

The Dutch got over the first of these handicaps by challenging the English at sea; she turned the second to her own advantage; but she could do nothing about her endemic lack of home-grown timber, and the disagreements appeared insoluble.

The first Dutch War (1652–4) broke out over English flag discrimination to safeguard her own shipping, compounded by the enforcement of a deliberate act of obeisance demanding that all ships of foreign powers must salute all English ships – sovereignty in the Narrow Seas. The tide of success flowed to and fro, with the final advantage going to the English at the Battle of Scheveningen in 1653 when the Dutch were blockaded and their great commander Maarten Tromp was killed.

We know more about the ships of the Dutch Wars period than any of their predecessors because records were kept, models were made, and modern marine archaeology has resulted in the recovery of wrecks in surprisingly intact condition, notably the *Wasa* at Stockholm. They confirm that there was little to choose in the fighting quality of a galleon of the Dutch Wars and a ship-of-the-line of the Napoleonic Wars 150 years later. Until the coming of steam and steel and high-explosive in the second quarter of the nineteenth century, the fighting ship's configuration changed only in detail.

The *Zeven Provincien* was launched at Delft-shaven in 1665, the first year of the Second Dutch War. She was of 1,400 tons, described as 'swift and graceful', and a perfect example of the best of Dutch shipbuilding. Like all Dutch galleons she carried her guns in only two tiers and had a lighter draught than her English contemporaries, which gave her the same nippier advantage over the English ships as the *Ark Royal* had enjoyed over the Spanish galleons. She also had a much squarer stern, the characteristic Dutch straight sides instead of the prominent tumble-home of English ships, and a marked upward thrust of her beakhead. Also by contrast with the *Ark Royal* she had an even leaner appearance and only vestigial fore and after castles. She was manned by a crew of about 500, and was at once selected by the Dutch commander-in-chief Michiel Adriaanszoon de Ruyter.

Very little went right for the Dutch during the first year of the second war with England. While de Ruyter was absent on a distant operation, the Dutch fleet was mauled off the Norfolk coast by Sir William Penn and the Duke of York, losing over 30 ships and with 6,000 men killed and taken prisoner. But the resilience and speedy shipbuilding capacity of the Dutch were remarkable, especially as their total population was less than that of London. By the early summer of 1666 de Ruyter could put to sea with 80 fighting ships with some 21,000 officers and men and a total of 4,500 guns; similar figures to those of the enemy.

The Four Days Battle of 1666 is one of the biggest, most remarkable and bloodiest naval engagements in history, extending in time from the morning of 1 June until the evening of the 4th and running from off the coast between Ostend and

Dunkirk to the Thames estuary. The fearless de Ruyter put to sea on 31 May flying his flag in the new *Zeven Provincien*. He had marginal superiority over the English fleet of Prince Rupert and George Monck, Duke of Albemarle, but if he could link up with his French allies he would be substantially superior.

It all began badly for the English due to interference from above, consistently fatal to the fortunes of the fleet throughout history but a seemingly incurable disease amongst higher command. Believing a false rumour that the French were proceeding up-Channel to join their allies, the English king ordered Prince Rupert to take his force of 24 ships to meet them, 'an error', as Admiral Mahan has written, 'exposing both divisions to be beaten separately'. Albemarle proceeded to sea in thick mist with only 56 sail to confront the Dutch fleet of 85. Moreover, the sea was so choppy that the English, on the windward side of the Dutch, were unable to open the ports of their lowest and biggest guns for fear of taking in water and capsizing.

A furious exchange of broadsides continued all through the afternoon of 1 June, the number of ships disabled, the acts of bravery and the numbers killed on both sides being equally numerous. One of the English flagships, the *Swiftsure*, bearing the flag of the brilliant 27-year-old Admiral Sir William Berkeley, was boarded from many quarters, and, hopelessly outnumbered and with few of his men left alive, the young flag officer fought hand to hand until shot through the throat at point-blank range. Two Dutch admirals also died before fighting ceased with the onset of darkness, and both sides lost ships captured or sunk. The young Tromp, the late Maarten's dare-devil but undisciplined son Cornelis, suffered great damage to his ship, and the *Zeven Provincien* was savagely treated.

It was a short and anxious night for Dutchmen and Englishmen alike. 'By three or four in the Morning', ran one contemporary English account, 'a small breeze of Wind sprang up at N. E. and at a Council of Flag-Officers, his Grace the Lord General [Albemarle] resolved to draw our Fleet into a Reer-line of Battel.' He did more than plan a radical and highly successful evolution. He put new heart into his outnumbered fleet. 'If we had dreaded the number of the enemy,' Albemarle told them, 'we should have fled. But though we are inferior to them in ships, we are in all things else superior ...

Let the enemy feel that though our fleet be divided, our spirit is entire … To be overcome is the fortune of war, but to fly is the fashion of coward. Do let us teach the world that Englishmen would rather be acquainted with death than fear.'

Sailing into the enemy in line ahead, Albemarle re-engaged de Ruyter as furiously as before. Although the Dutch now outnumbered the English nearly two-to-one, and were later reinforced by 16 more fresh ships from Holland, de Ruyter could make little impression on the English line as Albemarle protectively nursed his worst damaged ships away towards the English coast. The one English tragedy of this second day revealed again the advantage enjoyed by the lighter Dutch ships.

'At five we fell foul of the Galloper [sandbank]', wrote an English eyewitness, 'where the Royal Prince was grounded, and the Leeward Tide set us so far from her, that we could not lie by to relieve her. On the other side, the Dutch fell so fast upon her, and with their Fireships threatened the boarding of her, that she was forced to strike her Flag for quarter.' With the *Zeven Provincien*, the *Royal Prince* was one of the largest and newest ships taking part in the battle, and the loss of her and her admiral and men to the enemy was a grievous blow.

During the third exhausting day of almost continuous combat, the Dutch pursued the English closely in their retreat towards the shelter of the coast. The *Zeven Provincien* suffered so seriously that she fell farther and farther behind until she was out of the fighting altogether, and it was not until the fourth day that she was repaired sufficiently to re-engage. Like his opposing C.-in-C., de Ruyter now ordered his flag officers to his ship for a council of war, and to put new heart into them. 'You see the English?' he told his officers. 'In the last 3 days you have experienced the worst they can do. Now, with me, you must finish our work on this last day … Be men. Better to die than run like guilty rogues. Fight, or you rot in an English prison … The enemy is near. The time for words is past. Deeds must now talk.'

They needed all the courage and endurance that their commander's rhetoric could induce, for Prince Rupert's squadron of 25 more fresh ships had now at last joined Albemarle, and there was still no sign of the French. Incredible as it may seem, the engagement on this fourth day was as closely fought as ever although many of the men could scarcely stand for weariness. An observer on board the *Zeven Provincien* described the mêlée that developed.

> Thus we found ourselves in the midst
> of the English who, being attacked on
> both sides, were thrown into confusion
> and saw their whole order destroyed, as
> well as by dint of the action as by the
> strong wind that was blowing. This was
> the hottest of the fight…

When a fog drew a merciful veil over the scene of carnage in the evening the advantage was with the Dutch. Both sides had suffered grievously but the English fleet was forced to retreat and their losses were marginally heavier.

The Comte de Guiche has left us a sharp-etched picture of the great de Ruyter onboard his flagship after the battle. 'I never saw him other than even-tempered, and when victory was assured, he said simply, "It is the good God that gives it to us." … He has something of the frankness and lack of polish of our patriarchs … The days after our victory I found him sweeping his own cabin and feeding his chickens.'

There was little time for the *Zeven Provincien* and the other badly mauled galleons to refit and repair. Before the end of the next month the English Admiralty had succeeded in deploying a massive fleet of more than 80 ships which sailed from the Thames under Albemarle and Rupert, again with the intention of destroying the Dutch fleet and seeking out convoys of merchantmen. This time the result was a disaster for the Dutch, and after losing 20 ships on St James's Day, 25 July, the *Zeven Provincien*, dismasted and under tow, limped back to port. The Dutch had been outgunned and outmanoeuvred from the start. Worse was to follow. A great convoy was discovered by the English at anchor in the Vlie river, and Admiral Sir Robert Holmes with a small detachment set about it to such effect that only some 20 ships out of almost 200 survived – an event that was flippantly referred to by the English for many years as 'Sir Robert Holmes, his Bonefire'.

After the disaster of St James's Day de Ruyter was certainly seen 'other than even-tempered'. His subordinate, young Tromp, had disobeyed orders and pursued a vendetta against a single English commander. It was not the first time he had left the line when most needed, and there was no love lost between the two admirals anyway. When Tromp came onboard the shattered and mastless *Zeven Provincien* de Ruyter gave him the sharp edge of his tongue in so loud a voice that all could hear as he accused Tromp of 'being a deserter'. Tromp gave as good as he got. But it was he who lost his command, and the government retained its faith in de Ruyter.

It was almost a year before de Ruyter gained his revenge against the English. London had suffered the twin disasters of the Great Plague and the Great Fire. Money was desperately short, and as an economy measure most of the fleet had been laid up, much of it in the River Medway near the mouth of the Thames. After completing preparations in great secrecy, an armada of some 100 ships mounting over 3,000 guns and manned by a total of more than 17,000 officers and men, including a strong force of troops, departed from Schoonveld on 4 June 1667. After a brief delay due to bad weather, de Ruyter dropped anchor in the King's Channel in the Thames estuary on 7 June. Here by prearrangement the senior military and naval officers were ferried to the *Zeven Provincien* in the dark and de Ruyter then explained in detail the complicated plans for an assault on the English ports and fleet.

In the early hours of 9 June a detached Dutch squadron began to move slowly up river while de Ruyter in the *Zeven Provincien* with the main body remained as reserve in the estuary. First the detached squadron bombarded Sheerness fort and then landed a party which captured the town. Panic was widespread. Vast numbers fled before what was thought to be a mass Dutch invasion. There was a run on the banks. The Secretary of the Navy himself, Samuel Pepys, believed the Navy Office and perhaps the nation was doomed. Like many others he panicked, withdrew what cash he could from the banks and sent his wife and father into the country with his valuables.

Only the Duke of Albemarle appeared capable of making any positive defence efforts. With the few remaining labourers he could summon to help, he stretched a cable across the Medway, sank some blockships and established guns on the shore. But the Dutch, now reinforced, made light of all this, smashed through the chain and brought up fireships which did their work with such efficiency that soon the smoke from burning vessels could be seen from Whitehall.

De Ruyter embarked from his flagship in a barge in order to supervise the work of destruction, which was going well when he arrived up the Medway. One laid-up galleon after another was fired. The greatest of all the English ships, the pride of the navy, the *Royal Charles*, which had conveyed King Charles II to Dover in 1660, was towed down river.

When there was no more destruction to commit in the Medway de Ruyter withdrew his barge, re-embarked in his flagship, and with an arrogant disregard for anything the English might do, raided up and down the Thames estuary at leisure, 'as dread a spectacle as ever Englishmen saw and a dishonour never to be wiped out', wrote another diarist of the day, John Evelyn. Rumours that the Dutch were here, there and everywhere flew about the land causing the Surveyor to the Navy Sir William Batten to exclaim, 'By God I think the Devil shits Dutchmen.'

In his own time and after brushing aside a half-hearted English attack with fireships de Ruyter sailed for home. He was greeted with national jubilation. What a triumph! What a hero! And the *Royal*

Charles, no less, as the greatest of all prizes! Here was the final humiliation of the enemy. Years later when she was finally broken up, her magnificent stern carving was stripped off her and can be seen to this day as a memento of 'the glorious operations in the river of Rochester in the year 1667'.

The assault on the Medway and the burning of the English navy led directly to the Peace of Breda in August 1667.

There is a footnote to the Medway operation concerning de Ruyter and his flagship. At one point when he was tempted to proceed up the Thames and attack London itself, an English river pilot who claimed he knew every channel and current, was brought on board and offered his services to pilot them to the Tower. It is said that de Ruyter responded in icy tones, 'If you are so brave as you represent yourself to be, I will send you back again to your master King Charles, who has need of such valiant fellows as you.' Then he turned his back on the would-be traitor. In fact de Ruyter might well have proceeded farther if the promised French support had shown up. It never did. The French fought with both sides and with equal ineffectiveness during the Dutch Wars.

The peace lasted five years. Naval hostilities were reopened at the Battle of Solebay on 27 May 1672, an inconclusive affair of now traditional bloodiness at which de Ruyter again flew his flag in the *Zeven Provincien*. At Schoonveld de Ruyter proved himself the greatest admiral of his day. The regard with which he was held by both sides was expressed by a young English lieutenant rescued from the sea and permitted to watch de Ruyter conducting the remainder of the battle. 'Yes, he *is* an admiral', he is said to have exclaimed later, 'an admiral, a captain, a pilot, a soldier, a sailor! This man, this hero, is all of them in one!'

At length the fighting petered out, with English and Dutch antagonism growing greater against the French, whom they both regarded as perfidious and cowardly allies, than against one another. On 27 May 1674, with the two nations at peace, the *Zeven Provincien* sailed into Dover harbour to the sound of a gun salute from the castle and from the English ships. As soon as she dropped anchor English sailors swarmed onboard to pay homage to this great ship which had been fought so often and so gallantly against them. On these decks their fierce and brilliant adversary, Admiral Michiel de Ruyter, had directed so many actions, and had survived every danger.

The *Zeven Provincien*'s last battles were at Barfleur and La Hogue against the French, and with the English now as allies. The old ship again lost many killed and suffered grievous damage. She was broken up in 1694 after a fighting career of almost 30 years.

Bonhomme Richard

Frigate, 1766, USA

By contrast with most great fighting ships the *Bonhomme Richard* achieved fame in one fight which she won but, unlike her adversary, did not survive. She was an undistinguished vessel already past her best and was not even built as a fighting ship. Her claim to distinction stems from other causes.

The summer of 1778 was a season of exasperation and discontent for the American naval officer Captain John Paul Jones USN. This 31-year-old Scot, christened John Paul, a fugitive from a murder charge for killing in self-defence, and a convert to American citizenship, had been despatched in 1777 to France in command of the sloop *Ranger*. His orders were to 'distress' the British, and by his own definition 'to put an end of burnings in America by making a good fire in England of *Shipping*'.

Captain Jones's cruise with an insubordinate ship's company was a strictly limited material success, but a landing in Scotland and a raid on the English port of Whitehaven, bungled though it had been, caused all the 'distress' he could have hoped for, and widespread alarm and even panic followed it.

You have heard o' Paul Jones?
Have you not? Have you not?
And you've heard o' Paul Jones?
Have you not?

A rogue and a vagabond
Is he not? Is he not?
(bis)

Thus ran the opening verses of a long poem, one of a number chanted with terror and relish by English schoolchildren. From Jones's view the best result of this raid was not the trail of fear he left behind him but the satisfaction of capturing numerous English sailors who could be exchanged for American sailors languishing in English prisons.

On his return to France, Jones had visited Paris and there met Benjamin Franklin, Commissioner of the American Colonies. The two men at once struck up a friendship based on mutual admiration. The powerful Franklin became Jones's sponsor and unofficial patron. The *Ranger* had been ordered back to America without her commander, and for months Jones sought for a new ship to continue his depredations, but without success in spite of Franklin's strong support. Jones was never a man at ease with himself at the best of times and felt that the world misused him. Brilliant sailor he certainly was, and a consummately brave fighter, but even through his years of fame he never rid himself of the chips on his shoulder as the son of a gardener. He had made enemies of the Americans in Paris, and as a result saw one attractive command after another slip through his fingers. 'I beseech you,' he was reduced to exclaiming to the American Commissioners in August 1778, 'I conjure you, I demand of you to afford me Redress.'

It was not until November that the opportunity of acquiring a ship came his way. She was an old East Indiaman of doubtful quality called *Le Duc de Duras*. In spite of his eagerness to get to sea again Jones at first cast his canny eye over her doubtfully. 'I wish to have no Connection with any Ship that does not sail *fast*', he had once stated. Would she be fast enough? And was she too old and rotten? But when he heard that the King, 'in consequence of the distinguished manner in which you have served the United States', would place the East Indiaman at his disposal he jumped at the opportunity. Jones was at first given a wide-open brief. He could modify and arm the ship as he pleased, operate her where and how he thought best, could even choose a new name for her. Jones, in gratitude to his patron, selected the name *Bonhomme Richard* after Franklin's famous almanacs, *Les Maximes du Bonhomme Richard*.

Very little authenticated information is available on one of America's most famous fighting ships. Reasonably accurate deductions can, however, be made by comparing her with her contemporary French East Indiamen as they were all very similar in dimensions and rig. Almost certainly she registered between 850 and 1,000 tons, measured about 145 feet long with a beam of around 35 feet. Jones would have to modify her radically. In appearance and size she was similar to a contemporary French frigate and was to prove herself well able to stand up to the most modern of this class of fighting ship, although she could never be made to 'sail *fast*'.

Even the briefest and most superficial descriptions of her are rare. A Scotsman who went onboard after her conversion described her as Spanish or French built because of her apron bow. And 'she had three boats and a Norway Shaft [type of boat] belonging to her, one of which boats was out, and armed with four Serwivels [swivel guns] & Small Arms...' Later examination after her battle with the *Serapis* revealed the timbers of her lower deck 'greatly decayed with age'. Doubtless there was extensive decay elsewhere too.

Jones's first preoccupation was with the ship's armament. Cannon were hard to come by and it took him many weeks of travel and persuasion before he succeeded in gathering a mixed and sometimes old battery of 28 x 12-pounders, 6 x 9-pounders and 6 x 18-pounders, for which new ports had to be pierced in the side of the ship. Radical modification to the ship's interior had also to be carried out in order to accommodate for raiding purposes a contingent of soldiers and their officers.

As the weeks went by the confidence in the success of the cruise grew and Franco-American opinion came to regard it as a major operation. The main reason for this was the proposed invasion of England by a force of 20,000 to which Jones's operation would act as a diversion. It would be his duty to spread alarm and draw off troops to Scotland and northern England.

The new American-built frigate *Alliance*, more formidable than the *Bonhomme Richard* herself, was assigned to Jones's squadron, along with the French government's offering of the frigate *Pallas*, the brig *Vengeance* and a cutter *Le Cerf*. This force of five ships, if manned by ardent and disciplined crews and officered loyally and skilfully, could have been a great embarrassment to the British, a large part of whose navy was operating on the other side of the Atlantic. Unhappily Jones's squadron was marked by discord. The captain of the *Alliance*, Pierre Landais, was unbalanced. Most people thought he was mad. All the crews were unreliable. Ten different nationalities were represented in the *Bonhomme Richard*, many of them British deserters or prisoners-of-war, French fishermen and released convicts. But with the help of carefully chosen officers Jones succeeded in welding the *Bonhomme*

Richard's company into a fine fighting force. It was very different in the other ships.

When the squadron proceeded to sea on 19 June on a shake-down cruise and to do temporary escort duty to a convoy, the *Alliance* failed to give way as she should have done during an evolution in a squall, with the result that the two ships collided, losing between them a mizzenmast and a bowsprit.

At length and after repairs, John Paul Jones's historic cruise set sail from Lorient on 14 August 1779. The squadron had acquired two additional vessels, unwanted by Jones because of their unreliability, the privateers *Monsieur* and *Granville*. This made a total of seven vessels with a complement of over 1,500 officers and men of many nations and many inclinations. For the purpose of this operation, which was to become one of the most profoundly important in naval history, the ex-Scots gardener's boy was granted the courtesy title of Commodore.

Before the departure of Commodore Jones in the *Bonhomme Richard*, John Adams visited the ship and reported on this 'ambitious and intriguing officer'. 'Eccentricities and Irregularities are to be expected from him', he continued, '—they are in his Character, they are visible in his Eyes. His voice is soft and still and small, his eye has keenness and Wildness and softness in it.'

The 'eccentricities and irregularities' applied not only to Jones. The whole squadron was infected with them to such a degree that for much of its progress the voyage bordered on chaos and confusion. Orders were disregarded, ships disappeared on errands of their own and rejoined at leisure or not at all. There was no set plan and very few people recognized the purpose of the operation and knew only that they were going to get what they could out of it, treating it as a sort of large-scale piratical operation.

Four days out of Lorient the *Monsieur* captured a prize, refused to share it out among the others as agreed and by the following day was over the horizon. Off the southern Irish coast events were so chaotic and bizarre that it seemed as if leprechauns had swum out on the tide from the Skelligs. In a flat calm Jones feared that the *Bonhomme Richard* would drift onto the rocks and ordered a boat lowered to row his ship clear. Unfortunately it was manned by Irishmen who preferred to return to the uncertainties of their homeland than the Commodore's flagship, and coxed by a sailor who had been flogged for some misdemeanour it headed for the shore. Another boat manned by two officers and nine men was lowered to pursue them just as an Irish fog blanketed ships and shore alike. Neither was ever seen again.

There seemed no end to the comings and goings onboard the flagship. The mad Captain Landais with two other French officers from the *Alliance* came onboard the *Bonhomme Richard* and began haranguing Jones 'in the most gross and insulting terms' because, it seemed, the Commodore had ordered the frigate not to pursue a possible prize. Then, in quick succession as the calm began to build up to a gale, the *Cerf* disappeared when sent in search of the two missing boats, the *Alliance* made off in another direction with the *Pallas*, the privateer *Granville* pursued a prize against orders and made off with her. Jones had lost more than half the vessels in his squadron, including his most powerful, before the operation had even begun, before a shot had been fired. Seemingly undismayed by these defections, Jones sailed north along the west coast of Ireland, past cliffs and headlands which had devoured so many ships of an earlier Armada against England in 1588.

From time to time *Alliance* and *Pallas* hove into sight and remained in company for as long as it pleased them, ignoring all signals. Jones continued round the north coast of Scotland, still with nothing but a prize or two to show for his labours of three weeks at sea and 'much weakened and embarrassed with prisoners' as a consequence. During the first days of September the *Bonhomme Richard*, with *Pallas* and *Vengeance* in company, were sailing down the east coast of Scotland. None of the officers, petty officers or men knew what their Commodore planned next for the reason that Jones had no idea either. After suffering many days of gale from 4 September, and remaining out of sight of land until the 13th, Jones ordered his two French captains onboard to plan an offensive.

It was a stormy meeting, with the Commodore intent on exacting revenge for the hurts done to American ports by the ruthless English, and the Frenchmen predictably interested only in loot. Jones wanted to attack and burn Leith, Edinburgh's port, but his captains refused to support him. Later, after much argument, Jones seized on the inspired idea of holding the town to £200,000 ransom against burning it to the ground. This, according to Jones, 'was now heard with attention'.

The three ships sailed into the Firth of Forth on 17 September and came almost within gunshot off Leith as they prepared to lower boats. Panic had already seized the citizens. Women and children had fled inland, while the younger men armed themselves with any weapon they could lay their hands on. But luck was once more against the bold Commodore. A westerly gale blew blew up and cast him clear out of the Forth, and the relieved citizens at length returned to their homes.

Jones shaped course south again with no new plan in mind, content to act as circumstances offered. He thought it might be productive to raid Newcastle-upon-Tyne to burn colliers and thus threaten London's winter fuel supplies, but nothing came of that except more alarm amongst the citizenry of the town, and of South Shields, and later of other ports down the Northumberland and Yorkshire coasts.

On the morning of 22 September the *Bonhomme Richard* was off Spurn Head at the mouth of the Humber, still spoiling for a fight but failing to raise any interest among the armed vessels inside the estuary. Jones had left the *Pallas* off Flamborough Head chasing prizes, and in the evening he sailed north again with the little *Vengeance* to try to find her. At midnight, quite by chance, Jones came up with the *Pallas*, and – wonder of wonders – Captain Landais and the *Alliance* which he had not seen for 14 days.

Was Jones's luck about to change? Indeed it was. At this moment when he was in greater strength and better heart than for a long time, lookouts reported a forest of masts to the north and standing in their direction. It was a Baltic convoy of no fewer than 41 sail, a prize beyond the dreams of the most predatory commerce raider.

As daylight broke off the Yorkshire coast the convoy turned rapidly through 16 points (reverse direction) off Flamborough Head while its escort stood off shore to cover its escape. The men o'war were the frigate *Serapis*, Captain Richard Pearson, and sloop *Countess of Scarborough*. Now a fight was inevitable. And upon its outcome must depend the fate of that valuable convoy.

In the momentous battle that was to develop, neither the *Countess of Scarborough* nor the *Pallas* would seriously count. The *Serapis*'s weight of broadside was only marginally greater than that of the *Bonhomme Richard*, but her 20 big 18-pounders greatly increased this advantage over the American ship. She was also faster than Jones's vessel, a new frigate, copper-bottomed, which gave her a knot or two advantage in speed. But if the *Alliance* chose to live up to her name and fight alongside her Commodore the *Serapis* would have little chance of survival.

It was in keeping with the tragi-comic nature of Jones's cruiser that when at 6 pm, after a long haul north in light breezes, he ordered the 'form line of battle' signal to be hoisted, the *Alliance* merely hauled her wind and departed from this scene of imminent action, and the *Pallas* and *Vengeance* sheered off too, leaving the *Bonhomme Richard* to fight it out with the *Countess of Scarborough* and this formidable and well-handled frigate.

At 6.30 pm, with the sun just set over Flamborough Head and the moon rising, the two antagonists were sailing side by side heading east, gun ports open and guns run out, sharpshooters with swivels and muskets in the fighting tops, Pearson and Jones on their respective quarterdecks, marines at the ready for boarding. The *Bonhomme Richard* was flying English colours. Pearson knew better but went through the formality, hailing 'What ship is that?'

'The *Princess Royal*,' answered Jones shamelessly.

'Where from?' A pause. 'Answer immediately or I shall be under the necessity of firing into you.'

Jones then ordered the British colours to be struck and the red, white and blue ensign to be raised in its place. As the first broadsides blasted out, the white glow of muzzle flash reflected on the sea and the smoke rose up between the two ships. It was an unhappy opening for the Commodore. Two of his 18-pounders blew up instead of discharging, killing their crews, and his other guns could not match the battering effect of the English 18-pounders. It soon became as evident to Jones that he could beat the English frigate only by boarding and hand-to-hand combat as it was evident to Pearson that he must avoid being boarded and rely on his superior gunpower to batter the *Bonhomme Richard* to pieces.

With no interference from the other ships present, the battle developed into a test of seamanship as much as gunnery. In the light breeze prevailing, the two ships manoeuvred ponderously to gain the more favourable position, struggling for headway, backing and filling, firing when occasion allowed from as close as 50 feet.

Jones's first attempt to board, from a disadvantageous position, was repulsed without difficulty and with losses. Pearson then attempted to cross the *Bonhomme Richard*'s bow to rake her, but having insufficient headway merely took the *Bonhomme Richard*'s bowsprit. In the brief lull which might have led to another attempt at boarding Pearson hailed Jones, 'Has your ship struck?' Jones's reply has since become a part of the folk lore of the US Navy. 'I have not yet begun to fight,' he is reported to have yelled defiantly at the Royal Navy captain.

A further exchange of broadsides when the ships cleared proved the *Serapis*'s superiority again. Then, with great cunning and assisted by a fair measure of luck, Jones managed to bring his sorely damaged ship into contact again with his adversary, driving his jib boom into the *Serapis*'s mizzenmast shrouds and then forcing the English ship round and hard alongside him, bow to stern. Eagerly the grappling irons were thrown out, and soon the two adversaries were fast linked like boxers in a clinch, each throwing stabbing punches at the other.

After the earlier explosion among the 18-pounders, the gun crews had abandoned the rest of these heavy cannon. By contrast, the *Serapis*'s 18-pounders were working terrible execution below decks in the *Bonhomme Richard*, knocking out all her main armament at such short range that the English gunners had to thrust their staves into the enemy's gun ports in order to reload.

On the upper decks it was a different story. Jones had not after all given the order to board. He judged that he could bring about the frigate's surrender without doing so, relying on his sharpshooters in the fighting tops and the French marines on deck to destroy the *Serapis* and her crew by fire, bullet, grenade and the fire from deck guns and swivel guns. Jones himself and his men in the tops, clinging precariously from the yards and shrouds hurling grenades and firing their muskets, supported by the murderous fire of the French marines, so devastated the upper deck of the *Serapis* that no one could stay alive on it, the fires were getting out of control, and the efforts of Pearson's men to cut clear the grappling lines all ended in death.

Darkness had fallen and this ferocious action was illuminated constantly by the fires in both ships, by the flash of cannon, and intermittently by the near-full moon shining down through the broken cloud. Below decks the *Bonhomme Richard* was becoming as untenable as above decks in the *Serapis*, and after two hours the pace of the combat had in no way slackened.

It was at this time that Captain Landais chose to enter the fray. His participation was brief but damaging. Slowly the *Alliance* circled the grappled ships and poured in full broadsides from her 12-pounders, raking first the bows and then the stern of the American ship, as a sort of lunatic gesture of personal spite and accompanied by the screams of the injured and dying and the protests of the survivors. The Frenchman took not the slightest notice, delivered one more devastating broadside and took himself away as sinisterly and unpredictably as he had come.

The time was 10 pm. Half an hour later, when most of Jones's men believed that they could not endure for much longer the incessant battering of their ship, the unexpected happened. Suddenly as a fire below worked towards the *Serapis*'s magazine and her mainmast tottered, shot through with double-headed 9-pounder shot fired probably by Jones personally, Captain Pearson tore down his colours. The firing died slowly, few believing that the fight could be over. Then a lieutenant from the *Bonhomme Richard* swung onboard the littered, bloody and battered deck of the English frigate and escorted Captain Pearson back to Commodore Jones.

Although exposed to enemy fire directly and frequently throughout the long battle, neither officer was even scratched, doubtless because orders had been given by these commanders to avoid firing at the other, both valuing the satisfaction now being enjoyed by Jones. After exchanging a few words, Jones led Pearson below to take wine with him; and elsewhere on both ships the work of clearing up and tending to the dead and wounded was begun.

The *Bonhomme Richard*'s battle and victory had been paralleled in miniature with the capture of the little English sloop *Countess of Scarborough* by the larger *Pallas*, bringing the Commodore a total of over 500 prisoners, 24 officers of the Royal Navy and two commanders. Of the two ships he had won *Serapis* was in much the worse shape. But even her condition, once her fires had been extinguished, was seen to be much better than that of the *Bonhomme Richard*: '…a person must have been an Eye Witness to form a Just idea of this tremendous scene of Carneg, Wreck and ruin that Every Where appeared,' wrote the Commodore himself.

During the remainder of the night the two battered protagonists were dragged apart and the mixed squadron consisting of the *Bonhomme Richard*, *Serapis*, *Pallas*, *Vengeance*, *Countess of Scarborough* and *Alliance* got under way and began to sail slowly east – surely the oddest polyglot and heterogeneous collection of friend and foe and lunatic neutral that has ever sailed from a scene of battle.

The following morning the *Bonhomme Richard* was still burning in a number of places, and the water was still gaining on the pumps. It was clear to everyone but Jones, who so ardently wished to sail back with his flag still flying in her, that the old ship could not be kept afloat much longer. On the following morning, 25 September, at 11 o'clock, with her wounded and crew safely removed, Jones witnessed 'with inexpressible grief, the last glimpse of the Bonhomme Richard'. She went down bow first into the North Sea.

The defeat of the *Serapis* was of negligible importance to the strength of the Royal Navy and a small price to pay for succeeding in her primary duty which was to save her convoy. Commodore Jones returned with fewer ships than he had set out with. Nor did he at first return to France but to neutral Holland. His rebellious captains decided this for him, and as they had most of the prisoners Jones had willy-nilly to follow them into the Texel. Here, to his chagrin, he was obliged to remain, for tortuous diplomatic reasons, for the remainder of the year. Not until April 1780 did Jones reach Paris – to be received as another American hero was welcomed 147 years later; though Lindbergh made the journey quicker.

In any other year than 1779, when the cause of France and the USA was not prospering, in any other context than the struggle for independence of a small but potentially super-powerful nation, the action between the *Serapis* and the *Bonhomme Richard* would qualify for only a footnote in history, a skilfully conducted and heroically fought ship-to-ship action in which the weaker ship triumphed.

That it grew from a footnote to a notable volume, leather-bound and giltblocked at that, was the result of accident and the undeniably heroic style of John Paul Jones, a David-extraordinary defeating Goliath, a freedom-loving challenger to tyrannical arrogance, a symbol of defiance against impossible odds, and as ripe for heroic status as Leonidas at Thermopylae.

Every navy needs honoured occasions and honoured heroes upon which to build its tradition and pride. John Paul Jones provided both at the right time and in the right manner. His elaborate and revered tomb in the US Naval Academy does this remarkable hero due credit. John Paul Jones and the *Bonhomme Richard* with which his name will be linked for all time have fired the imaginations of Americans and inspired them with pride for 200 years. There is no higher ideal to which a sailor and his ship can aspire.

Victory

Ship-of-the-line, 1778, Britain

During the 100 years that separated the completion of the *Zeven Provincien* and the *Victory*, the
big fighting ship developed only in detail although
its size was considerably increased and the hitting-
power of a first-rate[1] in the Napoleonic wars was
much greater than a two-decker of the Anglo–
Dutch wars. France led the way in warship design
in the eighteenth century. The reforming zeal of
the Duc de Choiseul extended far beyond the
construction of new and the strengthening of old
bases and improvements in the training and educa-
tion of officers and men. Choiseul appointed ship
architects like Coulomb and Ollivier, and the fine
tradition of French ship design and construction led
to vessels like the 74-gun two-decker ships-of-the-
line of the 1770s, fast, responsive sailers, capable of

bringing all their lower heavy guns to bear even in heavy seas.

These 74s were as highly prized in the Royal Navy as muskets by the early Indians. When one was captured and sailed under British colours the combination of British seamanship, esprit de corps and gunnery with French design made an almost invincible fighting unit.

French first-rates, great three-deckers mounting as many as 110 guns, were equally superior. Outwardly, however, there was little to distinguish French, Spanish, Dutch and British ships that fought during the last decade of the eighteenth century and the first years of the nineteenth century. Compared with the *Zeven Provincien* and her contemporaries the most marked difference lay in the absence of rake. Any lingering remains of a forecastle had quite disappeared, although the name has remained to this day. The quarterdeck and the poop abaft the mizzenmast scarcely broke the ship's now almost level silhouette. The fourth mast had long since disappeared, adding further to the grace of the profile, and the rig was greatly simplified although spritsail and spritsail topsail were still sometimes carried as a sop to the traditionalists.

Only in the shape of the bows did there appear to have been a reactionary trend, resembling as they did the old rounded bluff form of the fifteenth century. There were two reasons for this. First, this configuration allowed a greater number of guns to bear on either bow, and second, it kept the ship drier in a head sea. The marked tumblehome remained, its bulgy purpose to compensate for the unbalancing effect of the heavy gun batteries.

The *Victory*, today still the flagship of the C.-in-C. at Portsmouth, was already 40 years old from her keel-laying by the time of Trafalgar, the battle that has made her one of the most famous ships in history, and this reflects her very high qualities at a time when English marine architecture was not at its best. But she is typical of her generation in most respects and her statistics are close to those of numerous first-rates. Her overall length, figurehead to taffrail, is 226' 6", the length of her keel 152' 3", and her extreme beam 51' 10". Her displacement is 2,162 tons.

The *Victory*'s main armament consists of 30 x 32-pounders with a range of $1\frac{1}{2}$ miles (though rarely fired at this distance from the target) and capable of penetrating three feet of solid oak at point-blank range, which was not an unusual range. The crew of 15 men to a gun could complete the arduous, complicated and fearsomely noisy process of cleaning, reloading and ramming with powder and 32-pound shot, running out and securing and firing (by flintlock now) in about one minute.

Slightly less destructive are the 28 x 24-pounders on the middle gun deck. Above them on the upper gun deck are 30 x 12-pounders, while on the fore-castle and quarterdeck are 14 more 12-pounders. A pair of 68-pounder carronades were effective only at short range but their nickname 'smashers' hints at the destruction they wreaked.

The ship's company consisted of some 850 officers and men, a similar complement to a twentieth-century battle cruiser of eight times the tonnage. Conditions were therefore very cramped and primitive for all but the senior officers, and the ship was often at sea for months on end. But standards of hygiene and health greatly improved during the lifetime of the *Victory*, and Nelson's flag-captain, Hardy, would never have tolerated a dirty ship. Discipline and punishments were equally ferocious, however, and the food appalling by present-day standards. But the commanders of the day succeeded in welding their rough, tough and often criminal men, few of whom had chosen the life, into an efficient and formidable fighting team. Prize money was always an important consideration, but a strong element of patriotism and proper hatred and contempt for the enemy coursed strongly through these sailors' veins.

–

The keel of the *Victory* was laid down at Chatham on 23 July 1759 in the dry dock, 'Old Single Dock'. It was of 20-inch-square teak guarded from injury by a false keel of five-inch elm. Stem and stern posts, the latter made of a single tree, were built up, and then the great ribs, the most difficult timber of all to find. By the time she had been completed at a cost of nearly £58,000 she had consumed 300,000 cubic feet of mature timber, a veritable forest of good English oak. Wars and the threat of wars were depleting English timber reserves at a rate that would soon have completely exhausted supplies: the steel ship arrived in the nick of time, for an oak tree requires a century of growth before it becomes usable.

Today in her dry dock at Portsmouth it is possible to study almost every corner of this great fighting ship. Expert guides will take the visitor below decks, explaining the identity and functions of everything, and with a certain relish the punishment procedures and the reason why the deck where the surgeon operated is painted red.

The first impression of the ship is as striking as of a giant nuclear-powered aircraft carrier of the 1970s. Of course there are the romantic associations of history and heroism which strike a deep chord. But the physical dimensions – the soaring height of the three masts, the unexpectedly long bowsprit, the sheer bulk of that oak hull – are awe-inspiring.

Yet no product of man could be more functional than this ship, seen from the outside or from below decks. Everything from the capstan with its 14 bar sockets, doubling as stores for first aid in battle, to the men's hammocks which, when not in use, are lashed up and stowed in the nettings for convenience, hygiene and splinter protection when in action, has a purpose or multi-purpose. The visitor has the impression that everything has been worked out economically, skilfully and as a result of long experience, so that this ship, with no power other than the wind and men's muscles, can weigh her great anchors (140 manpower), hoist sail, and travel to the other end of the world through whatever conditions are ordained by God.

It is all massive, masculine and tough below decks, and 'hearts of oak' takes on its literal meaning. And how small these sailors must have been! Today even a half-grown child has to watch his head. And short as we know Nelson to have been, could he really have accommodated his wound-racked body in that diminutive cot?

Then imagine the sights and sounds on the main gundeck in action, the gun teams functioning in marvellous co-ordination on the sanded and often bloody deck, every man aware that every round fired increased his chance of survival, the guns thrashing to and fro on their lashed mountings, recoiling with terrible violence on the instant of the equally terrible report. The scurrying powder monkeys with their lethal charges. The cursing and shouting. The smoke and fumes. The wounded and dying.

In the operational career of the *Victory* is reflected all the rigours and endurance, the chances, the endeavours, the triumphs that marked the dangerous and finally victorious years of the Royal Navy's second golden age. Her actions and admirals provide her with her own roll of honour.

It has been the fate of numerous fighting ships laid down in the heat of war to remain languishing on the stocks in the subsequent peace. The *Victory's* keel was laid down during the Seven Years' War (1756–63) but that war was almost forgotten by halfway through the later War of American Independence when the *Victory* was finally commissioned for the first time in 1778.

One of the first references to the *Victory's* fighting career occurs in the same year when, as Augustus Keppel's flagship of the Channel Fleet, the French ship *Licorne* was captured and brought to him. A month later at the engagement off Ushant, English party politics intervened in the action, Keppel's second-in-command. Sir Hugh Palliser, a strong Tory, playing a too muted part in the engagement – or so the convinced Whig Keppel would have it. (Both admirals were later court-martialled.)

Richard Kempenfelt and Lord Howe in turn hoisted their flag in the *Victory*, Howe's boldness and cunning leading to the relief of Gibraltar in the face of a much superior Franco-Spanish force.

Ten years later on the outbreak of the French Revolution the *Victory* became the flagship of another renowned admiral, Lord Hood, who occupied Toulon in the dangerous year of 1793. Hood left the command in November of the following year, and it was not until Sir John Jervis hoisted his flag on 3 December 1795 that the ship enjoyed a worthy flag officer again.

This was a time of harsher testing for the Royal Navy than at any time until 1940–1 when it again fought tyranny alone. Napoleon had overwhelmed Holland with its powerful naval forces – one icebound Dutch squadron actually being captured by cavalry. Spain declared war on Britain nine months later, leaving the British Admiralty to deal with three great naval powers at once.

In the Mediterranean Britain was outnumbered four-to-one, and yet the increasing adverse odds seemed to temper ever sharper the blade edge of British self-confidence and determination. There was one and one only reason for this: leadership.

Nelson, flying his broad pennant in the *Captain*, claimed that the Mediterranean Fleet was capable of achieving 'any and *everything*. Of all fleets I ever saw, I never saw one in point of officers and men to our present one, and with a commander-in-chief fit to lead them to glory'.

This high note of optimism found no echo at home. To his chagrin – and to Nelson's even more – Jervis was ordered to quit the Mediterranean at the end of 1796, entering the friendly Tagus from which Medina Sidonia had sailed to crush England 200 years earlier, in the *Victory* on 22 December. His total of ships ready for action had been reduced to nine. What could he hope to achieve against the mighty French and Spanish navies with such a token force?

Jervis's first responsibility in the new year was to prevent a Spanish fleet of 27 ships-of-the-line including many of the most powerful in the world, and commanded by Admiral Don José de Cordova, from linking up with Admiral Villeneuve's French fleet in Brest, which was poised to open the way for an invasion of England or Ireland.

Jervis had meanwhile been reinforced by six more ships-of-the-line fresh from England and was lying off Cape St Vincent, that rocky projection in south-west Portugal whence Henry the Navigator's caravels had sailed to seek a way to the East more than 300 years earlier. When the Dons' were sighted in two scattered and disordered groups, Jervis ordered his force of scarcely more than half their number to form line ahead and sail between them, splitting them even wider apart.

There took place onboard Jervis's flagship at this moment a conversation that crisply spells out British naval self-confidence and all that is meant by the invincible will to win.

'There are eight sail-of-the-line, Sir John,' Jervis was informed.

'Very well, sir,' he replied.

'There are twenty sail-of-the-line, Sir John,' corrected the captain of the fleet.

'Very well, sir.'

'There are twenty-seven sail-of-the-line, Sir John.'

'Enough, sir,' responded Sir John Jervis a trifle irritably, 'no more of that. The die is cast, and if there are fifty sail I will go through them.'

Conditions were difficult and Jervis's timing imperfect so that it appeared that the windward division of the enemy might make its escape before the English fleet could turn and engage the Spanish rear. At this point Nelson took matters into his own hands and without orders left the line and cut across to intercept the fast disappearing Spanish van.

In the furious engagement that followed Nelson placed the shattered *Captain* alongside one Spanish ship, boarded her and used her as a short route to board her even bigger consort beyond, the 112-gun *San Josef*. It was an action demanding immense courage in man-to-man fighting against vast odds and waggishly defined as his 'patent bridge for capturing enemies'. The battle earned him a knighthood and a nervous warning from his wife. Four of the Spanish ships were taken, the rest fleeing in disorder for the shelter of Cadiz, and the danger of invasion was temporarily averted.

It was not until May 1803 that Nelson, now a viscount and vice-admiral, the victor of the Nile and Camperdown and England's hero, hoisted his flag in the *Victory*. As his life accelerated towards its epochal climax some 30 months later he was to leave her decks for only brief intervals. Here was the most famous association of commander and fighting ship in naval history.

Britain was in even more acute danger of invasion than at the time of the clash off Cape St Vincent. As C.-in-C. of the Mediterranean Fleet it was Nelson's task to watch the French fleet under Admiral Pierre Villeneuve in Toulon and prevent its juncture with the Spanish fleet. It was as important for a great commander to possess endurance as it was to inspire his men, outmanoeuvre the enemy and show physical courage. Patience in full measure was demanded of Nelson and his commanders as, for month after month, they blockaded Toulon. A line of frigates kept close watch, the *Victory* and Nelson's other big ships remaining out of sight of land – 'those far distant, storm-beaten ships', as the American Admiral Mahan called them, 'upon which the Grand Army never looked' but which 'stood between it and the dominion of the world'.

Never was the strength and meaning of sea power more sharply demonstrated, never were hardship and boredom so manfully endured. Villeneuve got out once when a storm blew Nelson's frigates off station, but by good fortune for Nelson the French admiral was forced back into his own harbour. Three months later Villeneuve tried again and this time broke free from Nelson's grip and succeeded in sailing past Gibraltar into the Atlantic.

The *Victory* led the fleet of 12 ships-of-the-line in a desperate pursuit clear across the Atlantic, Nelson being guided by instinct and reports of varying reliability of Villeneuve's whereabouts. The fact that the French commander flitted about the Caribbean like a will-o'-the-wisp rather than face a force of scarcely more than half his strength shows the moral ascendancy Nelson had by now acquired. Villeneuve slipped away in obedience to orders to rendezvous with other naval squadrons from Mediterranean and Atlantic ports. Emperor Napoleon intended that his admiral should then gain temporary command of the Channel long enough for his armies to cross it and conquer the island.

Villeneuve was foiled by an English squadron off Ferrol, losing two of his ships, and seeking security and additional strength in Cadiz where the powerful Spanish fleet was already present.

Events now shaped themselves in classic style. Having satisfied himself that one of his 'band of brothers', the stalwart Cuthbert Collingwood, was watching the Spanish port, Nelson sailed the *Victory* home to Portsmouth for consultations in Whitehall and a last visit to his beloved Emma and their daughter at Merton.

Then, after letting it be known that 'I think I shall have to beat them yet,' he took the coach to Portsmouth where the *Victory* lay awaiting his return.

Never since Drake had embarked in the *Revenge* to meet the Spanish Armada had a flagship set sail with so many and such ardent prayers for victory as when England's greatest naval hero made his way down the steps to his barge, a small, frail, disabled, deeply troubled man who was yet sublimely confident of his own destiny. A great crowd, the women weeping, the men cheering, saw him off, knowing that the survival of the nation once again rested on his shoulders. People knelt and touched his uniform as he passed as if he were some new messiah. The date was 15 September 1805.

On 4 December the *Victory*, showing the scars of her greatest fight, came within sight of English shores again. Onboard she carried the corpse of 'the Hero', preserved in brandy and bearing the fatal wound of the bullet which had lodged close to his spine. 'It is a distressing sight', wrote the *Victory*'s flag-captain Thomas Masterman Hardy, 'to now see the Ships, Flags and Pendants half Mast on the melancholy occasion.'

Horatio Nelson's flagship had led the world's most efficient and destructive fleet against a combined foe superior in numbers, the signal 'England expects that every man will do his duty' flying from her halyards. They did so to such effect that in the ferocious, pell–mell Battle of Trafalgar, in which once again Nelson eschewed orthodoxy and sundered the enemy's line, he destroyed the enemy's spirit. At the end of the day 18 of the combined fleet's 33 vessels had been captured or destroyed.

Nelson was dead but Britain was saved from Napoleon's Grand Army which, as a direct consequence of defeat at sea, was itself to succumb ten years later on the field of Waterloo.

Essex

Frigate, 1799, USA

'The loss of several Vessels belonging to this Town', ran a letter in the *Salem Gazette* in June 1797, 'has given a serious alarm to our Merchants.' As America increased her trade she was reluctantly forced to recognize that it would need to be defended. It was not just the Barbary pirates who were giving trouble. Renewed war between France and Britain brought new insults to the American flag and losses of ships. There were few seas where unarmed merchantmen could sail in security.

The construction of the first United States peacetime navy led to much contention. Many citizens argued that the nation could not afford it. They also argued that even if they could a small navy would be worse than nothing. But losses continued to multiply and the demands of traders and seamen alike forced Congress to take action. On 27 March 1794 it passed by a narrow majority an act authorizing the construction or purchase of six men o'war.

In a memorable understatement the man made responsible for the design of these ships, the Quaker Joshua Humphreys of Philadelphia, wrote, 'As our navy for a considerable time will be inferior in numbers we are to consider what size ships will be most formidable and be an overmatch for those of an enemy.'

The result of his deliberations was a class of frigate, based partly on French and partly on clipper ship practice, which was unsurpassed until the end of the age of sail. The *Constitution*, *President*, *Chesapeake*, *United States*, *Congress* and *Constellation*, built in the last years of the eighteenth century, could even fight on equal terms with two-deckers. Their record added immeasurably to the foundations of self-confidence and esprit de corps established by John Paul Jones and his contemporaries in the War of Independence.

Clearly these frigates would be inadequate on their own to meet the need for protection of the growing American trading fleet, and it was Salem, the port that had suffered such heavy losses, that showed encouraging patriotism and free enterprise by building its own fighting ship.

No port in North America had a longer tradition of shipbuilding, the records going back to 1629; but the ships had been mainly small ones – brigs, fishing vessels, schooners and the like. In October 1798 subscribers of the town and neighbourhood met at the town hall where 'it was voted unanimously to build a *Frigate* of 32 guns, and loan the same to the Government'.

This ship was more modest in size than the *Constitution* and her sister ships. The frigate committee called in as designer and supervisor of construction Captain William Hackett, a man of uneven temper who from time to time, it was said, quite went off his head. Moreover he was an army not a naval captain. But he had inherited from his father John Hackett many skills and a fine shipyard in Salisbury. The committee's decision proved a sound one. Hackett Snr had designed and built the *Alliance*, John Paul Jones's troublesome consort during his most famous voyage. Many experienced seamen admired the fine lines, handling qualities and speed of that frigate, and the Salem frigate was to have dimensions and many characteristics similar to the unbalanced Captain Landais's old ship.

The papers covering every stage of the construction of the Salem frigate, to be named *Essex*, have survived and have recently been published in a splendid book (*see* Book List). The enthusiasm for the project is evident on every page and the reader can imagine the excitement that prevailed in the town.

The *Essex*'s keel was laid on 13 April 1799 in the yard of Enos Briggs on Winter Island. The timber was felled locally and brought in on sleds through the snow. Four months later the local newspaper was recording that 'the work on the Frigate building in this town is pushed with vigour. Connoisseurs say the ship looks well upon the stocks.'

Launching day on the last day of September turned into a gala festival. Schools closed and some 12,000 people crowded into the little town, jamming the roads with their carts. All the ships in the harbour dressed in their colours, and on the *Essex* herself main and foremasts were temporarily stepped to provide flagstaffs. As the blocks were moved cannon boomed out the federal salute, the stars and stripes were unfurled and there was a great roar of cheers from the nearby crowd and from those on the hills who were making a picnic of the event. 'There she goes!' came the cries; and it was reported that she 'went into the water with the most easy and graceful motion'.

In fact it had been a harrowing time for Captain Hackett and his worries were to continue until the frigate was commissioned. He was dependent upon widely scattered tradesmen for a multitude of materials. There are records of difficulties with Colonel Paul Revere (yes, *the* Paul Revere, now a successful metallurgist and founder) who could not keep pace with the demand for his noted 'Malable Copper' spikes because of the shortage of copper, and charged 50 cents a pound for them too. The rigging had to be worked up by McLennan and Sanders of Boston, the cannon were of English manufacture, the shot came from Benjamin Seymour of Plymouth, Massachusetts.

The copper sheathing provided by the navy, and only recently made a standard fitting as protection against *Teredo navalis* and as an enhancer of a ship's sailing qualities, came in 330 pieces and weighed in all 34 tons. The masts and spars had to be provided by other tradesmen.

After the launch the ship swarmed with joiners working on the interior, and her figurehead, which was to become so famous and was of an American Indian holding a tomahawk and with a single feather in his hair, was fitted. On 17 December 1799 she was complete and was duly presented to the United States Navy and accepted by 39-year-old Captain Edward Prebble, her first commander.

The *Essex* had cost the good people of Salem 74,000 dollars, but that was a very basic figure and did not include the cost of spare sails and masts, stores, armament, or even the expensive sheathing. With 12 months' stores onboard the total figure worked out at just 154,687 dollars.

She displaced 860 tons, the length of her keel was 118 feet and the height of her masts respectively 84, 77 and 72 feet. Her armament consisted of 26 x 12-pounders and 10 x 6-pounders, augmented according to the Salem records by 60 muskets and bayonets, 30 pairs of pistols, 100 boarding pikes and 100 cutlasses. Her complement was 250, including 60 able seamen, 73 ordinary seamen, 30 boys and 50 marines.

The Navy Department ordered the new frigate on her first operation without delay. She was to cruise with the frigate *Congress* to Batavia 'principally with the view of giving protection on the return voyage to a great number of vessels, and a vast amount of property our Merchants will have to come from thence about May next'.

The citizens of Salem, including the subscribers to the fund which paid for her construction, had only a brief opportunity to admire the vessel. The *Essex* sailed at dawn on Sunday 22 December. 'She fired a salute on going out', it was recounted, 'which was returned from Fort Pickering. She sailed remarkably well; and, from the abilities of her officers and crew, we anticipate a successful cruise.' The Essex's commander was delighted with her. 'The Essex is a good sea boat', he reported, 'and sailed remarkably fast. She went 11 miles per hour, with top gallant sail and within six points of the wind.'

—

The *Essex*'s active career, was to last some 14 years and was to be full of achievement. Under the command of Captain Prebble she completed her first assignment successfully and alone, the *Congress* meeting an early mishap and being forced to return. She was the first US Navy ship to double the Cape of Good Hope, and did so again when she returned with her large convoy.

She was back in American waters by November 1800, and was one of the units of a squadron of four men o'war under Commodore Richard Dale intended to put down the Barbary pirates who were making such depredations against American shipping in the Mediterranean. The *Essex* under the command of her new captain, William Bainbridge, arrived at Gibraltar on 1 July 1801 and made a rendezvous with the frigates *President* and *Philadelphia* and the schooner *Enterprise*.

The *Essex* began her escort duties without delay, convoying American trading vessels through the Mediterranean to the comparative safety of Gibraltar. With brief periods for repair and refit at Washington Navy Yard, she continued this arduous and often dangerous work until July 1806. On 27 April 1805 she was among the vessels which successfully attacked the town of Derne before peace with Tripoli was finally achieved and the

Mediterranean at last made comparatively safe for American merchantmen.

After troubles first with France and then Tripoli America now began to suffer a worsening of relations with Britain over obstruction of trade and a suspicion that Britain was inciting Indians to rebel against their masters. With the declaration of war in June 1812, the United States could not hope to challenge the mighty, invincible Royal Navy in a direct confrontation. But in a series of mainly individual ship-to-ship actions, notably the blowing up of the *Java* by the USS *Constitution* and the seizing of the *Macedonian* by the *United States*, the American navy disproved British claims to invincibility.

Other American frigates and smaller vessels played havoc with British shipping in distant seas, and none had a more spectacular career than the *Essex*.

–

After a comprehensive overhaul, the *Essex* had left her home port in October 1809 with despatches to His Majesty's Government relevant to the worsening relations between the two nations. Then again in January 1811 the frigate picked up the

American ambassador from Cowes, Isle of Wight. When war broke out she was at New York under the command of her last and most famous captain, David Porter. He was ordered to prey on enemy shipping in the Caribbean, doing so to such good effect that within a few weeks he returned with no fewer than 10 prizes, including the sloop *Alert*.

The *Essex* next joined the *Constitution* and the sloop *Hornet*, the three-ship squadron being under her old commander now Commodore William Bainbridge. New orders sent this detachment of American naval power into the South Atlantic in search of British East Indiamen returning with the riches of the East, just as English privateers had preyed on Spanish carracks 300 years earlier. They were also to 'act on discretion', and taking advantage of this Porter decided to extend his range even farther, double the Horn, and disrupt British trade in the Pacific with a special eye on the British whaling fleet. As the first American warship to double the Horn, and the first to sail Pacific waters, the *Essex* added further lustre to her name even before she seized her first prize.

The *Essex* fought her way round Cape Horn under appalling conditions, her company suffering greatly from the cold and lack of provisions. Her privations were eased by the seizure of two schooners, and she put in thankfully at the Chilean island of Mocha early in March 1813. She arrived at Valparaiso on 14 March.

The two schooners marked only the beginning of a mighty accumulation of enemy craft of many kinds which Porter seized over the following months among the Galapagos Islands and along the coasts of Central and South America. The British whaling industry was utterly destroyed by this single frigate. In all over 4,000 tons of shipping was captured or sent to the bottom and 400 Britons made prisoner. One of the larger prizes Porter converted into an armed cruiser, another of 355 tons he turned into a 20-gun sloop which he named *Essex Junior*.

When Porter decided that his frigate was in need of repairs and a refit, he sailed her 3,000 miles west to the Marquesas, cheekily claiming Madison Island for the USA, and using Nukuhiva as a base for repair work. It was as rewarding and enterprising a privateering cruise as any carried out by the French or English in earlier years, earned Porter a secure place in US Navy annals, and was a profound irritant to the British.

In the first days of 1814 the *Essex* with her '*Junior*' put in again at Valparaiso. The British had been conducting a desperate search for months for the raiders and they were at last to be rewarded with good fortune.

On 8 February 1814 the British frigate *Phoebe*, more heavily armed than the *Essex*, accompanied by the sloop *Cherub* and an armed storeship, sailed into Valparaiso harbour. James Hillyar, the *Phoebe*'s captain, brought his vessel provocatively close to the American frigate and then anchored to guard her in this neutral harbour. For seven weeks there was an armed suspicious truce between the enemy vessels with many taunts and counter-taunts being hurled between the crews.

Captain Porter, with ample time to assess the likely sailing qualities of his foes, became increasingly confident that the *Essex* could out-sail them. He also judged that it was only a matter of time before the British brought up reinforcements and that the arrival of another enemy ship must seal his fate.

On 28 March a strong southerly wind parted the *Essex*'s cables and Porter made a dash for the open sea. He was almost clear, with every prospect of showing a diminishing stern to the enemy, when his ship was struck by a sudden squall and lost her mainmast. The crash resulted in Porter losing his nerve, and he began to struggle back into the comparative security of the harbour. The wind was too strong for him and in the end he had to resort to anchoring close inshore three miles from Valparaiso.

If Hillyar had known of the severity of the fight he had on his hands he might not have sailed up to the crippled American with such confident relish, ensigns and flags fluttering in the fresh breeze. The *Phoebe*'s great gun superiority lay in her long 18-pounders which could outrange the *Essex*'s carronades. Hillyar opened fire with his long 18-pounders just after 4 pm, and throughout the engagement demonstrated a sensibly negative tactical policy. He had all the advantages and all the time in the world, and had no intention of unnecessarily wasting the lives of his men. Whenever it looked as if he might be damaged he drew off until he could strike again without danger.

Onboard the *Essex* was young Midshipman David Glasgow Farragut, the future famous admiral. He believed that the ship could have got away in spite of her disability. But now that the fight was on he conducted himself as bravely as the rest of Porter's men, and a great deal more bravely than a boatload who got away when things were at their hottest. He told later of a single gun being manned in turn by three crews as they were slaughtered, and of heroic self-sacrifice among the wounded.

As the hours wore on and the *Essex* became increasingly a shambles of splintered woodwork, torn rigging and wounded and dead men, Porter stood for the land in an attempt to run his ship ashore and burn her rather than strike his colours. He was foiled even in this by a freak shift of the wind. Soon after this he hoisted the white flag, recognizing at last that to persist in the unequal struggle could lead only to more slaughter. Eighty-nine of his men had already been killed in action or drowned, 66 more were wounded. The *Phoebe*, firing beyond the *Essex*'s range for almost the entire action, lost only four killed.

With good reason, Porter complained at the British frigate's violation of Chile's neutrality. With less justification he also sneered at Hillyar's caution throughout the fight. But the bitterness of his complaints was understandable under the circumstances. After one of the most successful and daring privateering cruises in history, to be battered to pieces off a foreign shore by superior forces was a hard experience.

The only consolation for Porter was that he and his surviving officers and men qualified for parole and could return to their native land. As for the poor battered *Essex*, the pride of Salem, she was jury-rigged and patched up and departed from Valparaiso on 4 August 1814. As HMS *Essex* she anchored in Plymouth Sound on 13 November.

The beautiful frigate deserved a less ignoble retirement. For nine years she was laid up, and then for more years served as a convict hulk. She was eventually auctioned off for £2,000, broken up and burned for the metal the patriots of Salem had paid for in 1799.

Monitor

Ironclad, 1862, USA

Half a century after Trafalgar was fought, three-decker ships-of-the-line with a configuration little different from the *Victory*'s were still being launched. 'Wooden walls', three masts and yards, fighting tops, beakhead, bowsprit – at a first glance nothing much seemed to have changed. But a second look revealed a single funnel amidships, surely an anachronism amongst all this inflammable rigging? An even closer look would identify guns far larger than those which had smashed Villen-euve's fleet – eight-inch shell guns whose projectiles could smash through any 'wooden wall' at a mile range and explode inside.

The introduction of shell-firing ordnance pres-aged a long contest between the skill and ingenuity of the steel manufacturer and the gunsmith, shell against armour plate. When the shell gun was harnessed efficiently with the steam engine, the era of the wind-driven fighting ship was at last over and a new concept of sea warfare was introduced.

The first radical move was made in 1858 by the French who ordered four frigates which were to be literally clad in iron. They were to be of 5,600 tons with their wooden hull plated to the upper deck with iron plates over four inches thick, backed by 26-inch-thick wood. Their announcement caused a great furore in Britain, and in the next year the Royal Navy laid down two much larger vessels, the *Warrior* and *Black Prince*, which went further than the *Gloire* and were actually built of iron.

For a long period after this revolution warship designers continued to provide for full sailing rig in addition to coal-fired boilers and reciprocating engines. In the Royal Navy it was for a while considered bad form to rely on your engines, which were noisy, dirty, extravagant and contrary to decent maritime practice.

Meanwhile the shell guns, grown now to as large as 112-pounders, were still mounted in the broad-side on two or three decks, although the notion was growing that this was ridiculously extravagant and provided the gunlayer with an unnecessarily large target.

With the invention of the turret, and the later demise of masts and rigging, the shape of the iron-clad and its successor, the Dreadnought, had at last been delineated.

Like most inventions, attribution for the turret is hedged around with counter-claims and dispute. The idea of securing one or more guns within a revolving cupola goes back into the grey mists of the eighteenth century and earlier. The introduction of the shell gun demanded greater protection for the gun crew as well as a smaller profile at which to aim. No doubt there were experiments in the 1850s in most naval nations, and the brilliant British naval captain, Cowper Coles, after experiments with armoured rafts, produced designs for a cupola ship carrying no fewer than 18 turrets. He got no encouragement from the Admiralty, only from Queen Victoria's much maligned, but percipient, husband, Prince Albert.

In the end credit must always go to the inventor whose design is first completed and made known to the world. In the case of the *Monitor* the turret gun was made and tested in battle and confirmed as successful under the stress of emergency in a remarkably short period.

John Ericsson, the *Monitor*'s designer, was born in Sweden and came to London in 1824 where he entered a locomotive design in the competition won by the Stephensons' 'Rocket'. Later he took a share in the prize for a workable screw propeller awarded by the Admiralty. He emigrated to America, became an American citizen and acquired a high reputation as an engineer and designer. He was an early pioneer in armour plate experiments for warships. When word was received that the Confederate Navy was converting a frigate into an ironclad, Ericsson was called in by Washington to provide a suitable answer to this threat.

The ingenious inventor, working on the principle of the smallest possible target with the lowest degree of vulnerability and the heaviest striking power, came up with a design that was a miniature caricature of the future seagoing ironclad battleship. Its influence had a startling effect on naval thinking everywhere. To old sea dogs who studied the drawings the end of the world had come, or at best gone insane.

Ericsson began by building a *submerged* hull with a flat bottom. Above it he placed an armoured raft. This allowed two feet of freeboard and no more. The secret of a raft's success is that the sea can wash over it at will – ask the *Kon-Tiki* men. Within this shell were housed an engine, an elaborate ventilating system with boilers, fuel, ammunition, and crew. Slap in the centre was the *raison d'être*, the Ericsson turret, armoured and rotated on a central spindle and surmounted by an equally invulnerable conning tower with narrow slits pierced in it. Within this citadel were mounted two 11-inch muzzle-loading guns.

It says much for the high morale of the navy that a crew could be found to man this nightmare of an iron floating tank. Moreover, under the command of a courageous Lieutenant Worden, this ship's company took Ericsson's *Monitor* out of New York and headed through – literally through – heavy seas under tow for Hampton Roads where the rebels were causing so much trouble. The tugs could not take it and had to put back. The *Monitor* struggled on, her crew half deafened and half asphyxiated.

Lieutenant Brooke of the Confederate Navy had taken a different approach to the design of his ironclad. He had raised the wreck of the frigate *Merrimack* from the bottom of the Norfolk Navy yard where she had been scuttled, burnt out and sunk. Below her old waterline everything seemed all right except for damaged engines. Onto her hull the lieutenant secured a thick sort of iron pot originally intended as a floating gun battery. Firing tests suggested that the new *Merrimack*, now renamed *Virginia*, was unsinkable.

This she proved herself to be on the morning of the day on which later the *Monitor* would clank and wallow her way into Hampton Roads.

The CSS *Virginia* caused consternation and havoc by steaming up to some enemy vessels, firing her considerable batteries, and ramming the Union sloop *Cumberland*. Full broadsides, shore battery fire, raking fire – nothing could produce any response from the ironclad except more shellfire from this grotesque parody of a ship. She then set about the frigate *Congress* and departed only when she was a blazing hulk.

When it was all over and a count was made of the damage, the Union commanders knew that the enemy would be back, the next day probably, to finish them off. They were right. But in the evening they welcomed the arrival of the equally bizarre reinforcement, the *Monitor*, half swamped below decks, its crew dazed and ill.

The duel between the *Monitor* and *Virginia* on 9 March 1862 can be compared with a group of boys in turn hurling stones at a saucepan lid and an upturned saucepan. It was a noisier business in Hampton Roads that day but only dents were made and personal injury was more or less limited to nosebleeds from the shock of impact. No more than superficial damage was done to either ship, and each withdrew, chastened, when out of ammunition or sufficient resolve to perpetuate the stalemate.

If any confirmation was still required to prove to the world that the sailing navies were now obsolete, the meeting of the *Virginia* with units of the Union sailing navy on 8 March and the *Monitor* on the following day provided it.

The *Monitor* gave her name to a class of fighting ship. The Union Navy rushed out more of them. Super-monitors were employed in numerous minor engagements in the nineteenth century, and as recently as 1944 15-inch-gunned monitors were used in the liberation of the Continent engagements.

The original *Monitor*'s life was as brief as it was notorious. She foundered off Cape Hatteras on 31 December 1862. It was a maritime miracle that she survived that long.

Mikasa

Battleship, 1902, Japan

After the revolution of warship design epitomized by the *Monitor*, the creative imagination of warship designers became sterile. These decades produced plenty of international crises, and even a minor naval war or two (Sino-Japanese, Spanish-American) but many years had passed since there had been a major battle between naval powers, and all conclusions were perforce theoretical. Not until the naval engagements between Russia and Japan in 1904–5, in which the victorious fleet was led by the flagship *Mikasa*, could any tangible lessons be drawn. For this reason alone (and there are others) *Mikasa* deserves a place in history.

When the decision was made in Japan to build up her armed forces and become a considerable world power, the authorities sensibly went to Germany to learn how to build an army, and to Britain for her naval ships and naval training. Through two decades British shipyards were kept busy building torpedo craft, cruisers and battleships for the new Imperial Japanese Navy. And very good ships they were too, serving the navy well in Japan's wars against China and Russia.

The *Mikasa*, laid down at Vickers' Barrow yard in 1899, was closely patterned on a whole generation of Royal Navy battleships of similar design and statistics, with a main armament of four heavy guns disposed in two turrets fore and aft, and a mixed secondary armament, all on a displacement of around 12,000–15,000 tons and with a speed of 15–18 knots. *Mikasa* on her completion could have joined the British Channel Fleet and no one could have noticed the difference. She did, in fact, enjoy rather higher figures in size and gunpower, displacing 15,000 tons, her 4 x 12-inch guns being supported by 14 x 6-inch, 20 x 12-pounders and numerous smaller guns for close action against torpedo attack. Fourteen-inch armour protected her barbettes, and 9-inch hardened steel protected her amidships. Her engines, in contemporary style, were reciprocating, and her 25 boilers were of course coal-fired. She did well on her speed trials, recording 18.6 knots.

Nothing could be less unorthodox than the *Mikasa*, yet her silhouette was pugnaciously purposeful. The great majority of her contemporaries led blameless and pacific lives. No such fate lay ahead for this battleship as she steamed for the first time into the Atlantic under the Japanese flag, heading for her distant home base.

The *Mikasa* is as synonymous with Admiral Heihachiro Togo as the *Victory* with Nelson. Togo, 'the father of the Japanese navy', had undergone much of his training in England. As commander of a small warship, he ordered the first shots to be fired in the Sino-Japanese war of 1894–5. He also fought in the Boxer rebellion of 1900. By the outbreak of hostilities with Russia in 1904 he had been promoted to C.-in-C. of the Japanese fleet, and the *Mikasa* remained his flagship for the duration of the war.

-

The final moves leading to war with Russia were made onboard the *Mikasa* on the morning of 6 February 1904 when 40 of the Japanese Navy's senior officers were assembled to listen to orders for a night attack on the Russian fleet at Port Arthur. The meeting ended with a toast to victory in champagne. Then the big battleship slipped her moorings and led the fleet to sea from Sasebo. By nightfall two days later the fleet was within 50 miles of the unsuspecting Russian fleet.

Just as the Japanese flagship remained beyond the horizon in the attack on Pearl Harbor 36 years later, so the *Mikasa* and the other Japanese heavy ships remained at a distance from the target area when the torpedo boats went in at midnight. The material results were below the Admiral's expectations. Only three torpedoes found their mark, but they were sufficient to disable temporarily two Russian battleships, and this just kept the balance of sea power in Japan's favour and allowed her to launch her invading troops safely across the sea.

The following morning the *Mikasa* steamed into action for the first time at the head of the First Division of six battleships and opened fire at 8,000 yards on the Russian ships and forts. This was a fine act of bravado and no doubt brought to white heat the fervour of Togo's officers and men. But for ships to challenge shore batteries has always been a dangerous business, and the *Mikasa* was soon receiving damaging hits. The cruisers which followed in the battleships' wake were the target for such furious fire that Togo had reluctantly to order retirement.

Port Arthur remained the key target for the Japanese fleet, and later for the army too, when the siege of the port began. Over the following weeks Togo brought his battleship division back several times to reopen the bombardment, but he recognized that until he could lure out and destroy at sea the damaged Russian fleet he had always to fear attacks on the sealanes between Japan and the mainland.

Togo enjoyed his first major victory two months later, although it was not in the glorious *banzai* tradition he would have preferred for the glory of his navy. Vice-Admiral Ossipovitch Makharov was provoked into bringing his battleships out of Port Arthur in pursuit of Japanese cruisers which had sunk one of his destroyers. On sighting the smoke of Togo's battleship division, however, the Russian Admiral retired hastily and incautiously over a Russian minefield. His flagship suddenly blew up, taking down with her the Admiral and 600 officers and men. A second battleship struck another mine a few minutes later, and although she managed to get back to her base, this loss in strength marked another savage blow against Russia. A month later, in this fateful tit-for-tat contest, Togo lost two of his six first-class battleships on mines, confirming the deadliness of these new weapons of sea warfare.

Togo now depended on his four remaining battleships and a strong force of modern armoured cruisers to retain control of the sea, a vital condition to the pursuit of the war. There was no possibility of adding to his strength, whereas the Russians had great reserves in European waters, including five new battleships ready or completing, which could be transferred to the Far East. In addition a Russian armoured cruiser squadron operating from Vladivostock was making increasing incursions on Japanese sea traffic. It was a time for a cool and steady hand on the conduct of the naval war, and the Japanese nation was supremely fortunate in possessing a C.-in-C. able to face such a situation.

On 10 August 1904 the new Russian naval commander at Port Arthur, Rear-Admiral Wilhelm Witgeft, took his fleet to sea with the intention of breaking through to Vladivostock. The safety of his ships was becoming increasingly threatened by the Japanese army's artillery, and it was decided that the northern base was preferable for operating against Japanese shipping.

This was the opportunity Togo had been awaiting for six months. On paper he was inferior in battleships and cruisers, but he had complete confidence in the fighting spirit and skill of his fleet, and like Nelson blockading Cadiz in 1805, he possessed the advantage of being already at sea, his men and ships in fighting trim.

By mid-morning the six big Russian battleships were seen steaming south-east into the Yellow Sea, a formidable line strongly supported by cruisers and destroyers, and with a hospital ship fatalistically taking station astern. Togo suffered an unpleasant shock when the distant twinkle of 12-inch gunfire at the unprecedented range of almost ten miles was followed half a minute later by huge waterspouts and the crash of exploding shells little more than 200 yards *on the far side* from the Russians. Many uncomfortable minutes passed before Togo could bring the *Mikasa*'s guns into range.

The battle on this hot, misty, calm day then developed into a series of elaborate evolutions at high speed, with the Russians attempting to break through the Japanese line and Togo manoeuvring to cut them off with the least possible damage to himself. But the *Mikasa* was badly hit just above the waterline at 13,000 yards, and it might have been the end of her if the sea had not been so calm. Then she was hit again on the deck forward and on her second funnel. Splinters whistled about Togo standing exposed on his bridge, wounding him slightly and causing him to be soaked by the blood of those about him who were killed. For a time it appeared that the Japanese might be facing disaster, and the loss of even a single big ship would be serious in view of the eventual arrival of Russian reinforcements from Europe.

Firing remained intermittent as the contestants closed and opened the range, and for a while there was a break for luncheon and a sorely needed rest from the heat of the battle and the summer sun. Hopes of what might well have been a Russian victory at sea, which would inevitably have led to a victory on land, were dashed when two 12-inch shells from the now much-reduced Japanese batteries struck the Russian flagship. One of these destroyed her foremast, the second killed almost all the Admiral's staff and Admiral Witgeft himself. It also blasted so many corpses against the wheel that the flagship began to turn sharply. This one shell turned the tide of battle and the shape of history. The Russian line fell into disorder and panic broke out.

Opportunism is one of the first qualities of a great admiral, and Togo showed his genius that afternoon by at once seizing the chance of adding to the panic and the damage he had already created. The *Mikasa* closed in, firing ever more accurately and with devastating effect. Statistically the advantage still lay with the Russians. In every other respect they were at a crippling disadvantage. Indecision prevailed for a long time after the C.-in-C.'s death, and when at last the second-in-command took the initiative it was only to give the order to retire back to Port Arthur, which inevitably meant a delayed death warrant for every vessel. A few of the smaller craft did in fact adhere to Witgeft's original order and attempted to break through to Vladivostock but all were either destroyed or driven into neutral ports. The main body of Russian battleships made off as fast as they could steam and in varying conditions humiliatingly came to anchor in the harbour from which they had been cheered out only hours earlier.

–

It was a disappointment to Togo that he had failed to sink a single ship at the Battle of August 10 and had left the responsibility for the destruction of the surviving Russian fleet to the army's howitzers. But he experienced great relief that the damage to his own ships was less serious than he had expected it might be after the first few minutes of the contest. The survival of the Japanese cause still rested on his four battleships and the very useful force of armoured cruisers. News had reached him that with the completion of the last of the new battleships in the Baltic, the Russian 2nd Pacific Squadron would sail for the East. Togo's own ships all required a thorough repair and refit before they would be ready for battle again. They had been steaming continuously since the outbreak of the war, boilers and guns needed radical attention, his men were in need of a rest.

Admiral Togo has been called a lucky admiral, the hit on the Russian flagship's conning tower has been called a lucky hit. In fact the misfortunes of the Russians, which proved so advantageous to the Japanese, were largely of their own doing; and that 12-inch shell struck exactly where any gunlayer would aim it to strike. The ineptitudes of the Russian naval command throughout the Russo-Japanese war were boundless, and nowhere more so than in the preparation of the reinforcement squadron and its despatch and journey to the Far East with orders to snatch back command of the sea from Togo. The delay in its departure and its long-drawn-out tragi-comic odyssey from Libau in the Baltic on 16 October 1904 to its arrival in the Far East seven months later provided Togo with the time he so desperately needed to get his ships back into fighting trim and make preparation for the reception of the enemy.

When Admiral Z. P. Rozhestvensky, C.-in-C. of the 2nd Pacific Squadron, led his mixed bag of warships – from modern battleships to aged coastal defence vessels and cruisers which had been returned from the Far East as obsolete decades earlier – half round the world to the war zone, he experienced every kind of hindrance. Almost at the outset the Admiral had ordered fire to be opened on some English fishing smacks in the North Sea on the bizarre calculation that they were Japanese torpedo boats. He was frequently denied ports for refuelling and provisioning, suffered mutinies, accidents, diplomatic intrigue and delaying tactics, sickness on a large scale, his own nervous breakdown, and in the end almost total demoralization.

The squadron straggled past Singapore on 8 April 1905, taking an hour to do so. By this time its misadventures were the wonder of the world. Considering the difficulties Rozhestvensky had had to face, it was extraordinary that he had even arrived. But to an experienced eye, his was not a fleet fit for battle with the efficient Togo in spite of its numbers. The ships' hulls were rusty and heavily barnacled from lying for weeks on end in tropical anchorages, and so deep in the water that armoured belts were almost below the waterline. Coal was piled everywhere on the decks and the impression of instability which was always evident in armoured ships of French design – as these largely were – was greatly reinforced. No British naval officer observing through glasses the passage of this extraordinary collection of men o'war would have cared to go into battle in any of them, least of all the flagship *Suvoroff*.

Togo calculated correctly that his foe would choose the short route to Vladivostock through the Straits of Tsu-Shima rather than the longer route round the Japanese islands, and had made meticulous scouting arrangements for all the sea approaches to be covered by cruisers and armed merchantmen equipped with wireless, the first time this new means of communication had been used in naval warfare. The *Mikasa* had been in dry dock during the winter and brought back to a state of 100 per cent efficiency by February. The battle fleet was anchored in Chin-Hei bay on the south-eastern coast of Korea, the Japanese navy's secret base for many months past. At exactly 5.15 am on the morning of 27 May 1905 a wireless sighting report was received cracklingly across the ether, repeated again and again in Morse. The Russian fleet had been glimpsed heading for the eastern entrance of the Tsu-Shima straits.

There was nothing ostentatious about Togo's cabin where he first received the news he had been awaiting for so long. There was a roll-top desk, a bowl of artificial flowers on the mantelpiece, dwarf flowers flanking the imitation fireplace, a painting by his steward of the bombardment of Port Arthur on one wall, and hanging from another wall a dud Russian shell which had struck the *Mikasa*'s bridge. Soon after dawn the Japanese fleet, the *Mikasa* as always proudly in the van, steamed out of the wide anchorage, staining the misty morning sky black with a great cloud of funnel smoke. Togo was being regularly informed of the progress and disposition of the enemy, and he knew precisely when he would meet the Russians and how he would conduct the battle.

Refusing the pleas of his staff to take shelter in the *Mikasa*'s armoured conning tower, Togo sighted the head of Rozhestvensky's armada from the open bridge of his flagship at 1.20 pm. The sea was choppy, causing spray to smudge the lenses of glasses and rangefinders; visibility was moderate. Like his hero Nelson, Togo was always prepared to embrace the unorthodox. With the enemy approaching on a north-east course fine on Togo's starboard bow, the *Mikasa* led the line through a 90° turn to starboard across the course of the advancing Russians, turned to port 15 minutes later, and then, as disdainful of enemy fire as Nelson at the opening of Trafalgar, turned his entire line in succession through 180° to bring it parallel with but ahead of the Russian line.

Fire was opened at the comparatively close range of 7,000 yards, and as at the 10 August engagement, the Russian gunnery was at first excellent. One of Togo's ships was forced out of line and others were damaged, including the *Mikasa*. Again Togo was injured, this time in the thigh by a splinter. It is said he did not even pause in his study of the Russians through his telescope.

Due to poor seamanship the Russian line began the engagement in a state of some confusion. As the battle progressed, Togo with his superiority in speed 'bent' the Russian line more and more onto an easterly course. Rozhestvensky on the other hand appeared paralysed in mind and body, simply watching wordlessly his 'T' being crossed and the Japanese closing in on his fleet, which now began to feel the weight of Togo's more numerous 8-inch guns. After giving the one instruction to deploy in a single line, which was never fully carried out anyway, Rozhestvensky failed to issue another order throughout the battle, seemingly gripped with the fatalistic knowledge that his fleet was doomed – as he had known all along it was doomed.

No effort was made to get behind the Japanese line, which could have led to fatal damage to Togo's rear. Instead, one by one the Russian ships were struck, set on fire, and capsized. The *Suvoroff* was hit again and again by heavy and medium calibre shells. As at the earlier battle, the flagship's conning tower was struck, splinters screaming through the narrow aperture, killing and maiming. Rozhestvensky was badly wounded. Later he was transferred from his shattered and burning flagship to a destroyer.

After the first half hour of battle not a single hit had been made on the Japanese ships. Sensing victory, Togo closed the range, pounding the surviving Russian battleships into a shambles.

By dusk the Russian fleet was crushed. Yet many ships still remained afloat. The Japanese revelled in night fighting and intermittently all through the hours of darkness the little Japanese destroyers and torpedo boats harried the Russian survivors. At dawn the following day the *Mikasa* led the fleet in a great rounding-up operation of the Russian ships still afloat. Piecemeal the Russians surrendered – the destroyer carrying the wounded admiral, the useless coast defence vessels, a shattered battleship or two. Three cruisers got away to the Philippines to be interned. Only a brace of destroyers made Vladivostock – two insignificant little vessels out of Rozhestvensky's great armada.

–

As surely as Trafalgar led to the defeat on land of Napoleon, so Tsu-Shima made inevitable the surrender of the Russian armies. On land the Japanese had conquered on every front, at dreadful cost in lives and at increasingly crippling financial expense. Japan's credit was running out and the world knew it. Both sides wanted peace, and Togo's victory at Tsu-Shima provided the same impulse to negotiate as the atomic bombs which prefaced Japan's suing for peace in 1945. The American President, Theodore Roosevelt, brought the two sides together at Portsmouth, New Hampshire. After the sacrifices of 15 months of ferocious warfare, Japan appeared to derive little advantage from her victory, and the jubilation following Togo's glorious mastery of the Russian bear turned to outrage and riots in the major Japanese cities.

The *Mikasa*, which had so frequently avoided catastrophe from mines or shells, met disaster soon after the end of hostilities. Togo had gone to

Tokyo from the naval base at Sasebo to congratulate the Emperor and celebrate the victory. The sailors remaining onboard had their own celebration, drinking toasts in industrial alcohol instead of champagne. To remove its smell they set fire to the last dregs, the flames got out of control, and the flagship blew up and sank, taking down 250 of her crew, just as if she had chosen a samurai's death in the face of the dishonourable peace her nation had been forced to accept by the great powers.

There is a happier postscript. The *Mikasa* was later raised and repaired and served honourably for many more years. Then, like Nelson's *Victory*, she was preserved as a national memorial at Yokosuka. Even the bombing of the Second World War did not touch her, and she survives to this day, the last example of her generation of ironclad battleship.

Von der Tann

Battle cruiser, 1910, Germany

The rise of the Imperial German Navy over a period of less than 20 years is one of the most remarkable creative and organizational accomplishments of modern times. The consequences of this birth of a new naval power were profound and its increasing strength was so politically inflammatory that it became the greatest single cause of the First World War.

In 1896 the German navy was an insignificant force of coastal defence and small vessels. Britannia ruled the waves, Germany ruled the land – that was how the average German citizen viewed the power-sharing of Europe. All this changed with the appointment in 1897 of Alfred von Tirpitz as head of the German navy. With the powerful support of the Kaiser himself, Emperor Wilhelm

II, Tirpitz succeeded in introducing two successive Navy Laws, in 1898 and 1900, providing for the building of a greatly enlarged ocean navy. The intention and definition were made clear to the world in a Prefatory memorandum to the 1900 Act: 'Germany must have a battle fleet so strong that, even for the adversary with the greatest sea power, a war against it would involve such dangers as to imperil his position in the world.'

Here was direct and provocative evidence that Britannia's rule of the waves was about to be challenged. In German eyes the time was ripe. With her acquisition of colonies across the world, her increase in wealth, trade and responsibilities, Imperial Germany must secure her sea communications as well as her land frontiers. German opinion, stung by Britain's arrogant stance over Africa and the Boer War – even apprehending German ships on the high seas – was ready to support this challenge to British naval dominance. Besides, the Kaiser had always been jealous of his grandmother's fleet, and this was no trivial consideration. As a final flourish and declaration of intent it would be called the High Seas Fleet.

Britain countered first by climbing down from aloof independence and signing treaties of friendship with Japan and France which eased her naval responsibilities in the Mediterranean and the Pacific; second by greatly accelerating her own naval rearmament. While from 1897 Tirpitz commanded the transformation of Germany into naval greatness, in Britain the vigorous and ruthless figure of Admiral John Arbuthnot Fisher masterminded the Royal Navy's reply to this challenge. He, too, had the heartfelt support of his sovereign, King Edward VII.

A new impetus to this battleship race was the rapid and secret construction by the British of a warship as revolutionary as the *Monitor*. When HMS *Dreadnought* was revealed to the world in 1906 she was regarded with consternation as well as acclaim. Here was a battleship which could outpace and outgun every battleship in the world. She could choose to fight, when she must destroy her adversary; or she could choose to retire, when she must survive to fight another day. Her innovations included turbine engines, speed over 21 knots, all-big-gun armament of 10 x 12-inch – most battleships carried four big guns.

Because she made every battleship in the world obsolete and Britain had the most, the *Dreadnought* and Fisher were subjected to much abuse at home. But the fact was, and Fisher had the secret, Germany was already far advanced with her own big ship plans. So were Japan and the USA for that matter. What Fisher had done was to steal a march on his opponents and gain moral and *matériel* ascendancy. Moreover, with her greater shipbuilding resources he knew that Britain could build a new all-Dreadnought fleet faster than Germany. He was right. He nearly always was.

'Jackie' Fisher's next trick was downright cheeky. Having astonished the world with the *Dreadnought* and while everyone was wondering and arguing, and Tirpitz was initiating a crash programme of German Dreadnought construction, Fisher presented the world with a new cruiser that was even more dramatically superior to every other cruiser than his battleship was to all existing battleships. Shortly before the *Dreadnought* was launched there was laid down, in even greater secrecy, a 17,000-ton vessel with a speed of 28 knots and a main armament of 8 x 12-inch guns, with the typical gutsy working title of HMS

Unapproachable. The previous class of armoured cruiser could steam at 23 knots (just), and had a mixed armament of 9.2-inch and 7.5-inch guns giving a broadside weight of shell less than half that of this new cruiser.

By the time she and two simultaneous sister ships were revealed to the world the German admiralty had known for some time that this new class of cruiser was going to be radically more powerful and faster than its predecessors. They therefore countered by laying down the biggest ever armoured cruiser, SMS *Blücher*. But German Intelligence had underestimated the statistics of the British ship. This armoured cruiser proved to be smaller and slower than its British counterpart, and its guns were of only 8.2-inch calibre, its broadside weight 2,560 pounds against 5,100.

Jackie Fisher, who loved making up and quoting aphorisms to underline his contentious beliefs, justified his giant new cruisers thus:

Tortoises were apportioned to *catch hares*.
Millions of tortoises can't catch a hare.
The Almighty arranged the greyhound to catch
the hare—

The greyhound so largely bigger than the hare
as to annihilate it…

The Invincible class of cruiser, soon formally to be called battle cruisers and informally by some 'ocean greyhounds', came as a nasty surprise to the German Admiralty, for here was a trio of British ships all completed before the *Blücher*, which could scout ahead of the fleet, destroy enemy scouting ships, retire rapidly on locating the enemy; and, in a different role, pursue, overtake and overwhelm any commerce raiders anywhere in the world.

When she was commissioned in 1910 the German second reply to this new class of British cruiser justified all the shrewd and careful thought the design team put into her. The characteristics of the *Von der Tann*, the first of nine battle cruisers Germany built for two world wars, held tenaciously to the principles laid down by Tirpitz. This great admiral believed that the first priority in heavy warship design was protection and that near-unsinkability came before speed and firepower. A ship that might be battered to a gunless standstill in battle remained floating and repairable. A ship that went to the bottom was gone for ever, taking three years and a couple of million pounds to replace.

Germany's first Dreadnoughts were slower than the *Dreadnought* herself, packed a lighter broadside, were fitted with outmoded reciprocating engines, and were cramped to live in. But they were exceptionally tough. For years experiments were carried out to devise the most effective means of protecting a vessel from both shell and torpedo fire. 'Endless labour was expended upon details such as the pumping system or the possibility of speedily counteracting a list by flooding corresponding compartments,' wrote Tirpitz.

The depth of the armour plate was important, as was the internal subdivision of the ships, with numerous athwartships bulkheads reinforced by longitudinal bulkheads stretching almost from stem to stern and giving a honeycomb result with numerous watertight doors.

All this was sound architecture and marine engineering. But its emphasis on the importance of defensive qualities also influenced the basic thinking of German command towards a defensive outlook conditioned by caution. The belief in the paramount importance of the need to preserve the ship because of its cost, its wonderful complexity and the time and resources required to replace it was high among British commanders. It was higher still in the *Kreigsmarine*. In both navies there was a deep-seated fear of the unknown, i.e. the new weapons, the mine and torpedo. Soon it would be the aerial bomb.

When the statistics and photographs of the first German Dreadnoughts were made public in Britain there was scathing comment. The Royal Navy, it seemed, had no cause to fear these slow, undergunned battleships. Their beam figures and their stoutness, however, suggested to the more discerning eye that these were comprehensively protected ships. And so they proved to be. On countless occasions Tirpitz's insistence an his ships' protective qualities was justified. German heavy ships could be reduced almost to a shambles and still they would not sink.

The *Von der Tann* was built in the record German time of two and a half years, a reflection of the urgency with which she was needed by the navy. The British public had an opportunity of examining this first German battle cruiser closely when she was chosen to represent her service at the Coronation

Fleet review in 1911. She was low and handsome in a tough Teutonic style that was to become familiar to the sailors of two world wars. Her main armament was disposed as in the *Invincible* in four turrets, two *en echelon* amidships so that they could theoretically be brought to bear through a narrow arc on both broadsides. Her guns were 11-inch. But the Krupp 11-inch was an efficient weapon with a very high muzzle velocity; and the secondary armament, intended primarily to ward off destroyer attack, was more powerful than the *Invincible*'s. She was reported to be very fast, almost as fast as the *Invincible*, and she was the first large German warship to be engined with turbines. Yes, a fine-looking vessel, Englishmen were saying. But no better than our battle cruisers, and we've got four already at sea…

The *Von der Tann*'s commander, Captain W. Zenker, was an exceptionally able and respected officer (he later became chief of staff to the navy). He brought his ship to a state of high efficiency which was admired throughout the fleet. The *Von der Tann*'s gunnery was especially brilliant, and she held for many years the much competed-for world record for coaling – 394 tons per hour – at a time when this was a largely manual and totally filthy business in which all the ship's company participated.

—

When war came three years later Germany had added five more to her battle cruiser strength, and the *Blücher* was tagged on to the First Scouting Group under Admiral Franz Hipper.

The battle cruiser forces of both the German High Seas Fleet and of the British Grand Fleet acquired the reputation of a *corps d'élite*. The ships were more heavily and frequently engaged than the battleship squadrons, which brushed only at Jutland, and suffered by far the worst casualties. Their speed combined with ferocious striking power and their role in the van in battle ensured them this glamorous reputation. From the very outset of hostilities they were in action and in the headlines. The Germans also had the battle cruiser *Goeben* in the Mediterranean, and her escape to Turkey, through her commander's skill and British ineptitude, had the most profound military and political consequences, strongly influencing Turkey to enter the war on the German side. In the same opening month of the war British battle cruisers operating deep in German waters in the Heligoland Bight and in support of British light forces, sank in short measure three enemy cruisers and a torpedo boat. In December and on the other side of the world the *Invincible* and *Inflexible*, supported by smaller craft temporarily detached from Admiral Beatty's command, all but wiped out a powerful commerce raiding force of six armoured and light cruisers off the Falkland Islands.

At this stage of the war the German High Seas Fleet had not distinguished itself, and the *Von der Tann*'s first actions were contemptible rather than materially damaging in the eyes of the enemy. German naval policy was to nibble at the superior strength of the British Grand Fleet by laying mines, attacking with submarines and contriving tactically to isolate and overwhelm inferior forces, with a special eye on the battle cruiser force, in an effort to equalize numbers.

On 3 November 1914 the *Von der Tann* and three of her consorts made lightning raids on the English east coast in order to cover the laying of a minefield. By way of a diversion, the battle cruisers attempted to bombard Yarmouth. The greater part of the High Seas Fleet was also at sea in the hope that the British battle cruisers might react.

A more elaborate and determined attempt to provoke Beatty and draw him into a trap took place on 16 December. The Germans were aware that Beatty was without three of his big ships and took advantage of this temporary loss by staging another vigorous raid, combining the operation with the laying of a minefield, over which they hoped to lure the British fleet. Again the main German fleet was in distant attendance, ready to sweep onto any inferior British force that might respond to the battle cruisers' presence.

Hipper's five battle cruisers (including the hybrid *Blücher*) closed the English coast at dawn and split into two groups, the *Von der Tann* and *Derfflinger* turning south to shell at close range the small English towns of Scarborough and Whitby. The other battle cruisers shelled Hartlepool, and in all 550 people were killed or wounded. While Hartlepool was defended by a few aged 6-inch guns, which actually made some hits so short was the range, the *Von der Tann*'s targets were undefended residential towns. This breaking of the Hague Convention and the deaths of so many civilians caused outrage, and not only in Britain. Hipper was especially vilified, and acquired for the rest of the war the soubriquet 'baby-killer'.

The Royal Navy came close to exacting payment for this outrage as the German First Scouting Group withdrew, the Admiralty having been alerted to the likelihood of the operation. Beatty and a detachment of battleships had sped south, and by a series of mischances missed Hipper's ships by only a hairsbreadth. It was not until 24 January that Beatty's luck changed in his favour. Perhaps luckily for the ship's company, the *Von der Tann* was in dock undergoing repairs following a collision. In a running fight in which only Beatty's flagship suffered serious material damage, the German flagship lost two of its heavy gun turrets, came close to blowing up and was in dockyard hands for two months; and the *Blücher* was sunk.

As a result of this defeat the German C.-in-C. was relieved of his command and was replaced by an even more cautious officer. There was then a long lull in naval action against Britain while the land war settled down to the bloody, near-static attrition which was to last for almost four more years.

The *Von der Tann* did not fire her guns again until August 1915. With two other battle cruisers she was sent into the Baltic and took part in several bombardments of Russian targets, this time of a more military nature.

A year after the change in command of the High Seas Fleet the C.- in-C. died and was succeeded by Admiral Reinhard Scheer, an able and more vigorous officer. An offensive spirit at once began to manifest itself in the German fleet. It was of vital importance to the German cause that the strength of the High Seas Fleet should not be endangered. It posed a constant threat to Britain and obliged her to allot a heavy proportion of total war effort to maintaining a vigil. Scheer believed it was still possible to commit irreparable damage to the British fleet without great risk to his own. He had the utmost faith in his ships and his men, and recognized what a fillip to their morale and to national morale generally a victory in the North Sea would be.

Scheer returned to the idea of a grand trap – a trap to snare Beatty's battle cruisers, which operated separately from the Grand Fleet's battleships and were more vulnerable to German gunfire. The plan was for Hipper to take his battle cruisers north across the North Sea and make his presence known off the coast of Norway, while a powerful force of U-boats was stationed to intercept Beatty's battle cruisers. Scheer's main force of battleships would be held over the horizon, ready to close in and destroy the thinskinned British ships before they could escape with their superior speed.

What Scheer and the German Admiralty did not know was that almost since the beginning of the war the British had been reading their signals, giving them the same advantage the American Navy was to enjoy in the Pacific 25 years later. By this means the Admiralty was able to warn both Admiral John Jellicoe, the British C.-in-C., and Beatty that the German fleet was probably putting to sea. Moreover the British possessed this Intelligence more than nine hours before Hipper actually led his battle cruisers out of the Jade estuary early on the morning of 31 May 1916.

Astern of Hipper, who flew his flag in the newest battle cruiser *Lützow*, steamed the *Derfflinger*, *Seydlitz*, *Moltke* and at the rear the oldest unit in the First Scouting Group, the *Von der Tann*. The Second Scouting Group which accompanied them consisted of five fast light cruisers and no fewer than

30 large torpedo boats of a kind the British called destroyers. Here, then, was the bait. The traps were first the U-boats, and then the 22 battleships of Scheer's fleet steaming 50 miles to the rear of the *Von der Tann*.

By dawn on 31 May a curious and unprecedented situation had developed in the North Sea. The Germans had good reason to believe that the British battle cruisers were at sea and heading in their direction and had no reason to believe that the British battleships were at sea. Their hopes of a crushing victory were therefore high. The British also had good reason to believe that the German battle cruisers were at sea and heading in their direction and every reason to believe that the German battleships were still in harbour. Their hopes of a crushing victory were therefore equally high. In short, both sides thought they might soon crush the enemy with overwhelming strength because they believed that the main battle fleet of the other was still safely in its base.

The British had prior warning of the German operation by superior Intelligence, but this was flawed by misinterpreting a signal suggesting that the battleships of the High Seas Fleet were not involved in this sortie. Both fleets were due to rendezvous in the early afternoon, the British rendezvous point being to the west of the German point.

Hipper and Beatty were heading for their points of rendezvous when their light scouting forces sighted each other and opened fire at 2.28 pm. The German and British battle cruisers hastened expectantly towards the sound of firing. Fifty minutes later Captain Zenker and the others on the bridge of the *Von der Tann* sighted six grey shapes speeding beneath a heavy pall of black smoke to the south-west. They were identified at once as Beatty's battle cruisers, led by the magnificently handsome *Lion*. They were on an easterly course. It was the first time that the ship's company had seen their adversaries in nearly two years of war. But now at last battle was inevitable, and it was satisfactory to Zenker and especially to his gunnery officers that they would have the great advantage of firing at the enemy against the brighter western light, while in the British rangefinders they would appear as much dimmer and less defined targets.

On sighting the enemy Hipper reversed the course of his battle cruisers to south-east in order to draw the unsuspecting Beatty onto Scheer's fleet out of sight to the south. As the *Von der Tann* completed her turn, heeling over heavily in the calm sea, Zenker saw that Beatty had also altered course to conform with their own. At 3.47 pm a series of yellow sparkles was observed on the *Lion*, and then within seconds all along the line of British ships. *Von der Tann* was under fire for the first time.

The first salvoes screamed overhead half a minute later and exploded far on their port side – a very long overshoot. If this was to be the standard of enemy shooting it seemed they had little to fear. The *Von der Tann* and the four ships ahead of her, steaming now at full speed like Beatty's ships, were quick to find the range, helped not only by the favourable light but by being on the lee side so that their cordite and funnel smoke was carried away to port. Their opponents had to peer through their own smoke as well as the smoke of their destroyers which had chosen this untimely moment to steam between the two lines to position themselves for an attack. *Von der Tann*'s target was the *Indefatigable*, also the rearmost ship and easily distinguishable from the earlier *Invincible* by the even spacing of her funnels.

Although Beatty had the advantage in numbers due to a signalling failure – the first of too many – the *Derfflinger* remained for a while free from the distraction of enemy attention, which helped her shooting. As the range closed right down to 12,000 yards the first hits were scored on both sides. The British flagship was suffering worst but every big ship present was being straddled and the quiet, calm, hazy afternoon had been transformed into a cacophony of firing and exploding shells and the scream of projectiles, while the sea erupted into countless, tall mushrooms of spray.

Zenker suddenly noted a flash on the British flagship followed by a glow as if a giant furnace door had opened amidships. For a moment it looked as if the *Lion* was going to blow up, but she steamed on at great speed, firing steadily at the *Lützow* and hitting her just before 4 pm.

The *Von der Tann*'s own shooting had now become very accurate and at 4.02 pm three out of a salvo of four of her shells struck the upper deck of the British battle cruiser. Zenker clearly observed an explosion through his binoculars and saw the *Indefatigable* haul out of line as if blasted off her course. The next salvo struck her on the fore turret. It was too much for the lightly protected ship. These hits were followed by a massive explosion and the battle cruiser disappeared with more than a thousand of her crew into the black cloud of her own funeral pyre. Thus did the speed and accuracy of the *Von der Tann*'s shooting pay off.

The chief gunnery officer ordered fire at once to be shifted to the *New Zealand*, now last in the British line, but before shooting began in earnest on this new target shells began falling about the *Von der Tann* from a fresh quarter, from far astern of the British line. Moreover the fire became almost at once highly accurate and the explosions greater than any they had so far experienced.[2] To the west Zenker could just make out four grey shapes, twin-funnelled ships shooting at a range they could not hope to match. He recognized them as the brand new super-Dreadnoughts of the Queen Elizabeth class mounting 15-inch guns, the biggest, fastest and most formidable battleships in the world. Having reduced the British to equal numbers the Germans now faced four more.

Within a few salvoes the *Von der Tann* was being straddled, and then came her first injury. A 15-inch shell struck her squarely, penetrating below the waterline. The sea came flooding in, some 700 tons of it. But no more. Her watertight bulkheads held and the big ship shook herself and steamed on at full speed, zig-zagging now to confuse the enemy gunlayers. Her own shooting at the *New Zealand* was becoming less steady as if the gun crews were beginning to tire. In fact in all the ships except the new arrivals the pace and heat of this gun duel which by 4.25 pm had lasted without a lull for nearly 50 minutes was beginning to tell on both gun crews and stokers working at full pitch in the confinement and hellish noise of their own trades.

The inevitable and terrible culmination came at 4.26 pm when the *Queen Mary* which had been suffering for some time the combined concentrated and accurate fire of the *Derfflinger* and *Seydlitz*, blew up. Her end was even more sudden than the *Indefatigable*'s. From the *Von der Tann* there could be seen a red flash near her third turret, another explosion forward and a third almost simultaneously amidships. Then there was nothing except a vast cloud of billowing smoke. Only a few men in the *Tiger* and *New Zealand*, whose ships had to alter course to avoid the worst of the falling debris, caught a glimpse of the 26,000-ton ship's stern thrust high out of the water, the propellers slowly revolving.

But by now the British 15-inch shells were doing serious damage to the German line. In a desperate endeavour to free himself from the forest of shell bursts Hipper ordered his torpedo boats into the attack. Beatty by coincidence made the same signal to his destroyers and within a short time there developed ferocious gun and torpedo combats between the two lines at ranges down to a third of a mile, while the big ships ceased fire and turned away from the threatening torpedoes in mutual relief.

In the *Von der Tann* from about 4.25 pm many of the ship's company were given the opportunity to rest, while others continued to toil in the engine rooms and set about repairing the damage and attending to the dead and wounded. Captain Zenker was well aware that the lull was likely to be brief. Soon both protagonists in the battle cruiser fleets must sight the main body of Scheer's battle fleet which he knew was hastening to their aid from the south. Then his ship would be expected to play its full part in completing the destruction of Beatty's ships.

The first indication that Scheer was in close proximity and that relief was therefore imminent was the distant view of the *Lion*, and then the others in succession, turning through 16 points to reverse their course. By 4.45 pm the tall masts of Scheer's battleships could be seen through the mist patches which had been growing denser and more frequent. The leading German battleships, the *König*, *Grosser Kurfürst* and the rest, were already opening fire.

The British ships in all their battered vulnerability were now the victims of the High Seas Fleet's trap. Or so it seemed; and it was no wonder that they were turning so hastily in the face of this overwhelming enemy power. At 4.57 pm the big 15-inch-gunned British battleships began to turn too, receiving hits again and again from Scheer's main force. They were returning the fire, though, and scoring hits themselves; but it seemed to those who witnessed this British turnabout that they must all be doomed.

At 4.52 the sorely battered *Lützow* started to turn through 16 points to renew the pursuit of the British ships, and the other battle cruisers, all more or less damaged, followed the flagship round onto a northwesterly course. Firing was at once renewed between the battle cruisers, with greater vigour than ever, and hits were soon again being made on the rearguard of Beatty's line, while the *Lion* concentrated her remaining guns on the *Von der Tann*.

The ding-dong gunnery duel, with damage to both sides, continued through the ever-decreasing visibility until at 5.10 pm fire ceased temporarily as neither side was able to see the other well enough. But the *Von der Tann* and her consorts remained in touch and exchanged damage with the 15-inch-gunned battleships until 5.30 pm. Then again there was a lull while Scheer endeavoured to close the gap and carry out the *coup de grâce* on the enemy. Neither Hipper nor Scheer, nor anyone in the German fleet as it steamed northwards firing at the fleeing enemy as opportunity occurred, could know that just over the horizon and steaming towards them at a closing speed of 36 knots was the whole might of the British Grand Fleet. The trap was about to close. But it was not a German trap, not this time.

The first hint of danger occurred at 5.56 pm. Suddenly heavy shells coming from a fresh bearing began exploding about the *Von der Tann*. The enemy was indeed, as the official German narrative later described it, as many-headed as a hydra. The German battle cruisers now turned away to the south-west to seek Scheer's support again, Hipper at the same time passing to his C.-in-C. the stunning news that they might well all be steaming into the jaws of the whole British fleet.

Six o'clock marked another turning point in this battle of pursuit and counter-pursuit. The full truth was now known to both sides. But it could be comprehended only in the broadest outline. Its edges were blurred by the frustrating patches of mist and the smoke from gun cordite, funnels and burning men o'war. It was therefore impossible to identify for sure the position, the course and strength of all the squadrons of no fewer than 64 big ships and nearly 200 cruisers and destroyers groping through the mist for each other over these few square miles of North Sea. The ether was crackling with signals telling of sightings. They were rarely accurate as to position, bearing or speed. A ship two miles away might be seen as a flash of gunfire, or a sudden ruddier glow as she was struck. A shape would loom up and be gone like a ghost before it could be recognized.

The last thing the German C.-in-C. wanted was to be confronted with the massed squadrons of British Dreadnoughts. He had been taken completely by surprise. Instead of facing the exciting and imminent prospect of destroying Beatty's heavy scouting force he had now to extricate himself from a highly dangerous position. The light might be bad but at high summer in this high latitude the evenings were long and it would be another three hours at least before he could benefit from the shelter of darkness. But first he had to be certain of the exact position of the enemy's main force before deciding on his own course of action.

Meanwhile, Zenker in the *Von der Tann* had taken station at the van of Scheer's battleships, which by 6 pm were tending towards a northeasterly course. There was the sound and flashes of intense firing ahead; and then suddenly out of the haze there loomed the shapes of four big armoured cruisers. Once again the *Von der Tann* opened fire and two of the enemy began to suffer hits both from the battle cruisers and the van of the battleships too. One of these armoured cruisers, the 14,000-ton *Defence*, blew up as the *Indefatigable* had done earlier, and another was seen limping into the mist, grievously damaged. She sank later.

But still there was no sign of Jellicoe's battleships, and it was not until 6.17 pm that heavy shells from yet another quarter suggested that all routes to the north, the east and west might now be closed to them. A few minutes later, intermittently through mist and smoke and all the more intimidating for the uncertainty of their strength and numbers, the characteristic tripod masts and heavy superstructures of British Dreadnoughts were sighted from the *Von der Tann*'s bridge. Muzzle flashes and the fall of shells about them – 12-inch, 13.5-inch and 15-inch – which in a few minutes seemed to stretch from horizon to horizon, confirmed the awesome truth that they were steaming directly at the crescent centre of the Grand Fleet.

Then, on this afternoon of surprises, and as the *Von der Tann* expected to be blown out of the water along with her fellow battle cruisers by a concentration of fire from 24 Dreadnoughts, three enemy battle cruisers appeared on their starboard quarter. They were the *Invincible*, *Inflexible* and *Indomitable*, all living up to their names by attempting to sweep down the vast side of the High Seas Fleet in order to cut off their escape route in that direction and still remain in touch with the enemy's van.

The turrets of the German battle cruisers that were still serviceable swung round and a brisk exchange of fire at once developed. At this range hits were inevitable. The *Invincible*'s firing was superb. Ahead of the *Von der Tann* the *Derfflinger* was again repeatedly hit, and Zenker suffered so many hits by 12-inch shell that all his heavy guns were put out of action. Suddenly the gallant *Invincible*, the first of 'the ocean greyhounds', failed to live up to her name after all. A heavy shell burst in one of her turrets and she instantly blew up. The fight was in shallow water, and after the vast cloud of smoke began to thin it was seen that this grandfather of all battle cruisers was standing up vertically out of the water in two pieces that were gravestones to her one thousand dead.

The High Seas Fleet escaped from the trap by turning simultaneously through 180 degrees – the *Kehrtwendung* – a manoeuvre under these circumstances requiring nerve and skill, and carried out so superbly that for a while Jellicoe and Beatty did not know where the enemy had gone.

As Hipper led his ships south-west out of the holocaust, he was forced to recognize the parlous condition of his Scouting Group. His flagship was deep in the water and would never get back to the Jade river; and he eventually transferred his flag to the *Moltke*, the least damaged of his ships. The condition of the *Derfflinger* was little better than that of the *Lützow*. In the *Von der Tann* Zenker was urging his men on to make serviceable at least one of his guns. It seemed highly unlikely that they would escape further action. This proved to be the case, and sooner than most commanders expected.

Scheer again reversed course, with the intention of taking his fleet north, east and south round the enemy and creeping back home down the Danish coast, at the same time sending in his torpedo boats to confuse and damage Jellicoe's battle fleet. It was an act of tactical despair, and it did not work. In the failing light and drifting smoke, Scheer with his battle cruisers now in the van again, found himself once more steaming straight into the centre of the enemy's line.

For several minutes, from 7.12 pm, the High Seas Fleet was subjected to a crushing barrage of shellfire from more than 120 heavy and many more lighter guns. Scheer had to balance the likely loss of the greater part of his fleet against deliberate sacrifice of the lesser part – his First Scouting Group, which appeared almost done for anyway. He chose the second course and ordered what came to be known (and according to the official British historian it was no exaggeration) as 'the death ride of the battle cruisers'.

With only a few guns able to fire, the five great ships which had seen almost continuous action for three and a half hours and had sunk four of the enemy's ships without loss, charged the British line to cover the battle fleet's second *Kehrtwendung*, with shells exploding all about them. After the gallant fight they had put up one could reasonably say they deserved a last-minute reprieve. As Scheer once again made off into the mist, this time in a very disordered state, he signalled to his Scouting Group 'to operate against the enemy van', which in effect allowed Hipper to turn south and then south-west to extricate himself.

Although Captain Zenker and his officers on the bridge of the battered *Von der Tann* could not know it, the main battle was over. There were skirmishes and alarums all through the night. The light forces clashed time and again, and at one dreadful moment a German battleship blew up with a searing flash from an enemy torpedo. But confusion and misunderstanding, poor signalling and inaccurate Intelligence on the British side allowed the mauled but still largely intact High Seas Fleet to evade Jellicoe and Beatty and reach the security of its base.

After struggling through the night to repair the worst of the damage. Captain Zenker's ship was the only German battle cruiser which could have defended herself by dawn. But Admiral Hipper had proved the strength of his ships and the courage and skill of his men. He had committed almost all the destruction and suffered by far the larger share of the damage. His flagship was at the bottom and all his other ships were in dockyard hands for the next two months, two of them until the following autumn, such was the battering they had received.

Before escaping from the superior might of the Grand Fleet Scheer had sunk more ships than his opponent. But within 48 hours of the end of the Battle of Jutland Jellicoe was able to report to the Admiralty that his fleet was ready for sea. Britain controlled the seas as firmly as after the more decisive and glorious Battle of Trafalgar, and the German fleet never seriously risked itself against the Grand Fleet, let alone challenged it in open battle.

The *Von der Tann* took part in several more sorties but her fighting war terminated with her magnificent performance at Jutland.

At noon on 19 November 1918 she followed the *Seydlitz*, *Moltke*, *Derfflinger* and the newest battle cruiser *Hindenburg* out of their base. She was, for the first time in her career, late in casting off, as if reluctant to undergo the humiliation of surrender. Later she met her rendezvous with the Grand Fleet and was led to the British base at Scapa Flow for internment. Seven months later, by secret orders to her crew, she pulled out her sea cocks and scuttled herself – at 2.15 pm on 21 June 1919, three years and three weeks after her finest hour.

Lion

Battle cruiser, 1912, Britain

Lieutenant Filson Young RNVR in the foretop of
HMS *Lion* at the first ever battle between big ships
in January 1915:

> To anyone sitting, as I was, on the
> target, surrounded by the enemy's shells,
> his shooting appeared to be painfully
> accurate; and, indeed, towards the end
> of the action, when two and possibly
> three ships were concentrating on the
> *Lion*, she was very nearly smothered by
> their fire. Sometimes from the foretop
> one could see the shell coming, a black
> speck in the smoky atmosphere, but
> gradually growing larger; in that case
> one knew that the direction of the

shot was accurate, exactly between one's eyes, and the only possibility of escape from it was that it should be either short or over...

In a naval war that was chiefly played out in unannounced and unrestricted attacks on merchantmen, and in the equally awful destruction of U-boats by the new processes of science, the battle cruiser actions of the First World War retained some of the traditional glory of sailing ship battles.

HMS *Invincible* and SMS *Von der Tann* had established the form of the battle cruiser. No ship more firmly set the seal on this speedy and crushingly destructive era of naval warfare than the *Lion*. She was the flagship of Sir David Beatty in the three chief operations in home waters in which battle cruisers participated. Twice seriously damaged in action, throughout the war she represented in British eyes the very essence of the fighting quality of the Grand Fleet. At the time of her completion in 1912 she was the largest and fastest warship ever built, and with her sister ships *Princess Royal* and *Queen Mary* provided a fast scouting and fighting wing of the fleet which, on paper, was invincible.

Not until 1916 did a German capital ship mount guns of larger calibre than 12-inch. 'My 4 pussy cats' as Beatty called the Lion class (with the 'one off' *Tiger*) were all operational in 1914 with 13.5-inch main armament.

As first completed in May 1912 the *Lion* had a purposeful but not altogether graceful profile, with her three funnels set irregularly and the curious disability of tripod mast and control top *abaft* the foremost funnel, thus risking the choking if not the incineration of key personnel at speed in battle when their services were most needed. (The same drawback was featured in numerous earlier British Dreadnoughts.) These fears were confirmed in high-speed trials. It took the common sense of a layman, Winston Churchill, recently installed in the Admiralty as First Lord, to stop this nonsense and re-position the mast where it ought to be and looked better.

The second design fault was more serious. By siting the third turret amidships the arc of fire was restricted to about 120° instead of some 350° if it had been superimposed above the fourth turret as the second was superimposed above the first. This potential loss of 25 per cent of the ship's broadside weight of shell was an inhibiting factor in the reckoning of any captain in manoeuvring and offset some of her advantage over her German contemporaries whose eight 12-inch guns could be brought to bear through all but the most fine angles.

In the Dreadnought era speed was one of the most expensive luxuries, an extra knot or two demanding extra boilers and extra bunkers for fuel, all of which added proportionally to the length of the hull, and thus the weight of armour to sheathe it, and thus the overall displacement, and thus the cost. When plans for the *Lion* were being prepared the latest German battle cruiser designs were for 25-knotters. The British Admiralty Board therefore asked for 27 knots for the *Lion*. In the event, while she just failed to make her designed speed, the German ships exceeded theirs by some three knots. By contrast with the most recent class of British battle cruiser the *Lion*'s displacement was up from 18,000 tons to 26,000; horsepower from 44,000 to 70,000; cost from £1.6m to £2.1m.

As for her protection, the *Lion* was better provided for than her predecessors, but there were flaws that were to prove fatal to one of her sisters and very nearly to herself. Although the main side belt maximum thickness was up from 6 inches to 9 inches, the horizontal protection against plunging fire from long range was totally inadequate. It is an unexplained anomaly in modern naval history that while gunmakers gave their ordnance ever greater range, navies consistently underestimated the range at which battles would be fought. In 1903 the accepted fighting range of battleships was 3,000 yards. In 1904 the Russians opened fire at the Japanese fleet at over 18,000 yards, news that was at first greeted with disbelief by the major naval powers. But why the astonishment when the ultimate range of modern naval guns was widely known? The *Lion* in peacetime never practised above 16,000 yards. At her first engagement with the German battle cruisers she opened fire at 20,000 yards. The consequence was that at both these engagements, in 1904 and 1915, ships were gravely damaged by plunging fire from shells falling from a steeper trajectory than was thought likely.

These faults in the *Lion* went unacknowledged in the public reception of the navy's greatest warship. She was extolled on all sides and even normally authoritative sources gave her speed on her trials over seven knots above the true figure.

She impressed her future enemy, too, and there was much public criticism at this time in Germany of the apparently inferior qualities of German designs. At full speed she was unquestionably a magnificent sight – a sight to intimidate any foe and reassure those who sailed her into battle.

In March 1913 Rear-Admiral Sir David Beatty hoisted his flag in the *Lion* as a prologue to his and the ship's most active and celebrated chapter. Beatty had been promoted to flag rank in 1910 at the age of 38, largely at the instigation of Admiral Prince Louis of Battenberg. He was the youngest flag officer for over a century. He was fearless, brilliant, stylish, the ideal officer to command this new breed of warship. The names of some ships are indissolubly linked with their commander or flag officer, from Drake with the *Golden Hind*, to Nelson with the *Victory*, to 'Bull' Halsey with the *Missouri*. Although like his flag-captain Ernie Chatfield, Beatty went on to the highest rank and to the highest appointment of all as Admiral of the Fleet and First Sea Lord, it was for those turbulent and sometimes dangerous years with the *Lion* that David Beatty will always be remembered.

On the outbreak of war on 4 August Beatty was already at sea with the First Battle Cruiser Squadron (it became 'Fleet' the following year), searching for the German fleet in case it contemplated a surprise raid. It was to be a long time before the Grand Fleet's battleships had the opportunity of getting to grips with the enemy, in spite of frequent provocative sweeps across the North Sea. Beatty's battle cruisers were to have better hunting.

The Battle of Heligoland Bight on 28 August 1914 was a demonstration to both sides of the complexity of modern sea warfare conducted at high speed in variable visibility and compounded by the threat of mines, torpedoes and long-range shore batteries. Poor staffwork, poor signalling and reporting, and weak tactics, were practised by the Germans and the British. What seemed likely to prove an unpleasant but not fatal defeat for British light forces was turned into a modest but important British victory by David Beatty flying his flag in the *Lion*.

British light cruisers and destroyers had put to sea to cut off enemy patrols deep inside the Heligoland Bight. Meeting inferior forces, they damaged and pursued them, while the Germans brought up fast cruiser reinforcements. The tide of the high-speed battle rapidly turned, and British ships were taking heavy punishment when out of the mist there loomed the great shape of the *Lion* and her consorts.

This sudden appearance of battle cruisers was as pleasant a surprise for the hard-pressed British, who had not been told, as it was unpleasant for the Germans. Beatty knew roughly what was going on in the Bight and had decided to risk the minefields and U-boats which were like teeth at the mouth of the German bases, and go in. With great rapidity and accurate fire, the *Lion* and the other battle cruisers sank every German ship in sight and retired before the German fleet could come to the rescue. Three German cruisers and a destroyer were sunk in the action without British loss. The material effect on the strength of the German fleet was not great. The moral effect was profound. It appeared to confirm once again that the Royal Navy was as invincible as in Nelson's day, a fact which the German naval authorities had always secretly feared. German self-confidence, a sensitive membrane in a nation lacking in maritime and naval tradition, was seriously damaged.

The battle cruiser squadron's incursion deep into German waters, and the damage it committed, for some time subdued the German navy's fighting spirit, and as Churchill put it, 'except for furtive movements ... not a dog stirred'. Later in the autumn of 1914 Admiral Franz von Hipper engaged in provocative raids himself, bombarding open towns, bringing British vilification upon himself and strong public criticism of the British Admiralty's seeming inability to intercept them and avenge the deaths of so many civilians.

It was not until 24 January 1915 that the balance was evened in an exciting running battle that showed again the pace and destructive power of Beatty's 'pussy cats'. Even Beatty, when he received orders on the afternoon of 23 January 1915 to prepare to sail at once, had no idea that the Admiralty with its priceless Intelligence breakthrough had prior knowledge that the German battle cruisers had been ordered out on a reconnaissance sweep towards the Dogger Bank.

A few hours later the *Lion* led the *Tiger*, *Princess Royal*, *New Zealand* and *Indomitable* under the towering girders of the Forth bridge and out into the North Sea. It was a clear, calm night with a slight breeze from the north-east. Filson Young tells us of that night of expectation and the following day of battle: 'For some curious reason', he wrote,

> we were confident on this occasion, in a way we had never been before, that we should meet the enemy on the morrow ... and there was an air of suppressed excitement which was very exhilarating ... The ship drove on calmly and stiffly through the dark surges. Midnight came, and with it the brief commotion incident on the changes of the watch; a slight aroma of cocoa was added to the other perfumes below deck, and I departed to turn in.

The *Lion* was to rendezvous with powerful and numerous light forces. Far to the north the main body of the Grand Fleet was hastening south to lend further steel to Beatty's force later if required. Shortly after 7 am, as daylight was breaking, the rendezvous was made, and 'the day was so clear', one officer recorded, 'that only the shape of the earth prevented one from seeing everything on it'. In the *Lion* the bugles sounded off action stations as flashes of gunfire rippled the southern horizon. 'Am in action with High Seas Fleet,' signalled one of the light scouting cruisers. Half an hour later a second cruiser signalled to *Lion*: 'Enemy sighted are 4 battle cruisers, speed 24 knots.'

Reassuring as this news was to Beatty, the message was incorrect in one important respect. The enemy's speed was more like 20 knots, and even when Hipper increased speed on recognizing the true nature of his adversary, he could find only another three more knots. Why was this when his flagship had recorded over 29 knots on high-speed trials? The reason lay in the decision to include in his Dreadnought battle cruiser force the *Blücher*.[3]

At 8.30 am the German battle cruisers which had smartly turned through 180° at 7.35 am and shaped course for their base on a southeasterly course were to the east of the *Lion*, fine on Beatty's port bow. The relative speeds were about 26 to 23 knots, the gap about 23,000 yards. It was as clear as the dawn sky that Hipper could not this time escape a gun duel and everything seemed to favour Beatty, even the wind which would blow his funnel and gun smoke clear while obscuring the enemy's sight of him.

Lieutenant Young recorded at 8.44 am, 'From the Lion's bridge the enemy appeared on the eastern horizon in the form of four separate wedges or triangles of smoke, with another mass of smoke ahead of them, coming from their destroyers. Suddenly from the rearmost of these wedges came a stab of white flame...'

This was an early sighting shot from the *Blücher* and it fell short. Beatty ordered 29 knots, beyond the capacity of any of his ships but a stimulant to stokers and engine room crews. The *Lion* spoke back with one 13.5-inch gun. Soon after 9 am in this classic stern chase the leading British ships and rearmost German ships were all in action. The *Lion* was hitting the *Blücher* and was herself steaming through a forest of tall waterspouts which were soaking her decks with spray. Every German ship was concentrating on Beatty's flagship, hoping to fend off the pursuit by destroying the enemy's van. She was being hit, too, and the strength of her armour plate was being sorely tested. But she was also returning the punishment. At 9.30 am one of her 13.5-inch shells struck the German flagship aft. 'There was no mistaking the difference between the bright, sharp stab of white flame that marked the firing of the enemy's guns, and this dull, glowing and fading glare.'

The hit nearly proved fatal to the *Seydlitz*. It ignited waiting charges in one turret and the flames spread down to the ammunition chamber. As the men opened the door to escape, the flames raged ahead of them, repeating the holocaust in the next turret, burning to death both gun crews – 159 men – and threatening the magazine itself, which was saved by flooding in the nick of time. The flames rose up 200 feet, convincing both Hipper and Beatty that the flagship was going up.

A misunderstood signal allotting targets left one of the German ships free of interference, and this ship was hitting the *Lion* time and again. On the other hand Beatty's ships were giving too much attention to the *Blücher* long after she was crippled and clearly out of the battle, although she continued gallantly to fire her guns to the end. Hipper was forced to leave her to her fate or risk the loss of his entire squadron.

This disaster became less likely when his policy of concentrating the greater part of his gunfire on the *Lion* began to pay off. Two heavy shells fell together on the British flagship and although her stout armour resisted penetration one of the shells dented it to such effect that water poured in, eventually putting her port engine out of action and giving her a 10° list. By 10.52 am she had lost all electric power, her wireless and signal searchlights were out of action, and by one of those freak chances of battle, most of her signal halyards had been shot away, which led to her mutilated signal to Rear-Admiral Moore to pursue the enemy with all despatch being misunderstood. To Beatty's fury and chagrin his largely undamaged battle cruisers gathered round the *Blücher* for the kill, something which could be accomplished by the supporting light forces. Hipper fled out of range.

What had promised to be a decisive victory under the most favourable circumstances was transformed in a few minutes of indecision and misunderstanding into a shambles – there is no other word for it. Beatty attempted to take up the fight again by transferring to a destroyer and thence to the *Princess Royal* at 12.20 pm. But by then even the most strenuous pursuit could not have brought Hipper within range before he reached the protection of his minefields and shore batteries.[4]

The lack of aggression and initiative in his subordinates privately dismayed Beatty but he breathed no word of public criticism. Sir John Fisher, the new First Sea Lord, in characteristic style wrote to Beatty, '*It is simply* ABSOLUTELY INCOMPREHENSIBLE *to me why Moore discontinued the action at* NOON!... WHAT POSSIBLE EXPLANATION IS THERE?'

The answer lay somewhere between blue funk and the reduction of initiative given to commanders in this new mechanized age of sea warfare, when a naval staff in London, far from the sight and sound and smell of battle issued tactical orders by wireless to their far-distant automata. Nothing could be better calculated to reduce the Nelsonian tradition of using your own head, laying alongside the enemy and disobeying orders if this could mean victory. 'In war the first principle is to disobey orders,' Fisher thundered. '*Any fool can obey orders!*'

In addition, the more complex and expensive warships became, the more reluctant were commanders to risk their ships. This 'cult of the *matériel*' did not exist in Nelson's day – this obsession with statistics of gun calibre and speed and armour penetration, and their glorification. It led commanders to avoid risking their ships in a way that would have been quite foreign to commanders in the French wars. The threat of the torpedo and mine further and understandably inhibited the spirit of risk-taking, when one chance mine could sink a ship costing around £100 million in today's money. Even Beatty suffered from it, and a sudden turn in the chase at Dogger Bank from a supposed U-boat had a bearing on his losing his quarry.

Beatty was deeply disappointed by the result. The gunnery of his squadron had been poor – just how poor he did not learn until later, for only the *Seydlitz* had been badly damaged, the *Moltke* was untouched. In all his five ships had made no more than two or three hits on the escaping battle cruisers, while the *Lion* had been hit by heavy shell 12 or 16 times (reports differ) and the *Tiger*, whose own shooting was abysmal, was hit six times.

–

But everyone else from Churchill and Jellicoe down appeared to regard the outcome as a victory, and a widely published photograph taken of the *Blücher* as she went down gave great general satisfaction. Beatty's stature as a national hero soared ever higher.

As to Beatty's flagship, it took two days to get the *Lion* safely home, surrounded by a screen of destroyers and towed by the *Indomitable*. Still listing heavily, the great ship with Beatty on the bridge acknowledging the cheering from the shore and the bridge above, passed slowly to her anchorage in the Forth. A few days later Churchill came onboard to congratulate her company. As he was leaving one of Beatty's captains drew him aside. 'Nelson has come again,' he said earnestly of his C.-in-C.

After the Dogger Bank engagement the *Lion* was out of action for four months. Exactly a year later, Beatty took her into the greatest of all her battles. No word of criticism could be aimed at the performance of the ship at the Battle of Jutland although she came as close as the *Seydlitz* at the Dogger Bank engagement to being blown up, and from the same cause. The ship took dreadful punishment, worse even than before, and 99 of her crew were killed, including the ship's chaplain who should have conducted the funeral service on the following morning.

On a lighter note, Beatty's biographer describes the contrasting conditions in a modern, tightly compartmented ship after a battle. When the officers descended to the wardroom again after passing through a shambles of twisted steel and broken pipes and torn deck, they found it exactly as it had been left just before tea time, with cups and saucers and plates of cakes and even vases of flowers set out on the table as if nothing of a disturbing nature had occurred onboard in the past 14 hours. On the other hand the navigating officer discovered that a heavy shell had passed clean through his cabin, its intense heat pulverizing everything except the steel heads of his golf clubs which lay, without handles or bag, in the corner where he had left them.

If the *Lion*'s performance at Jutland was beyond criticism, Beatty himself became reluctantly involved in the controversy between those officers who felt Jellicoe had let down Beatty and those who took the opposite view: an unhappy consequence of the less than satisfactory outcome from the British standpoint. It is an argument that will continue for ever. All that can be said here of Beatty's actions was that he fought with his pussy cats like a tiger, pursuing his foe relentlessly and with disregard for his own savage losses, and by brilliant manoeuvring succeeded in drawing the whole

German fleet into a trap that might have led to its wholesale destruction. If there was any failure on Beatty's part it was in the inadequacy of the information on the enemy's position and movements he passed to his C.-in-C.

Less than seven weeks later the *Lion* rejoined the battle cruiser fleet as flagship, a role of honour she retained to the end of her days. She participated in numerous North Sea sweeps, but only once (17 November 1917) came close to repeating her glorious performance at Jutland. By this time Beatty had succeeded Jellicoe as C.-in-C. Grand Fleet, and the *Lion* flew the flag of Vice-Admiral Pakenham. He was as bold an admiral as Beatty and had gained the respect of the Japanese at Tsu-Shima and other actions of the Russo-Japanese war by observing and taking notes while sitting on a deck-chair exposed to enemy fire throughout.

HMS *Lion*, ferocious pussy cat and most notable of battle cruisers, went to the wreckers' yard in 1924.

Warspite

Battleship, 1915, Britain

No modern battleship can boast as many superlatives as HMS *Warspite*, hero of two world wars, flagship of great commanders, victor in numerous great engagements from the Arctic to the Mediterranean. At Jutland the *Warspite* was one of the four great 15-inch-gun battleships of Admiral Sir Hugh Evan-Thomas's 5th Battle Squadron which brought succour to Admiral Sir David Beatty's hard-pressed battle cruisers. Her shells did great execution to numerous German ships until at a critical moment in the battle her helm jammed and she went into high-speed circles which brought her to within almost point-blank range of the main German battle fleet. Thirteen heavy shells struck her. But she escaped from this hail of fire and was ordered to retire from the battle. As she limped towards her base two torpedoes fired by a U-boat missed her by a hairsbreadth.

That afternoon in 1916 typified the extremes of fortune the *Warspite* experienced all through her life. It was characteristic that those two circles by chance encompassed a gravely damaged British armoured cruiser and allowed her to escape, thus saving countless lives. And those 13 hits by heavy shell killed only 13 ratings – and one officer – by contrast with the two or three hits on other big ships which blew them up, killing a thousand or more.

From 1915 until 1947, when she played her most whimsical trick of all, one never could tell with the *Warspite*. Like a great actress, one had to forgive her her temperamental ways.

By 1912 the Dreadnought era of all-big-gun capital ships was firmly established, the super-Dreadnought had succeeded the Dreadnought and the naval race between Britain and Germany – with other navies not so far behind – was at its hottest. 'Jackie' Fisher's iron rule at the British Admiralty was temporarily over and the professional head of the navy was the experienced and able Admiral Prince Louis of Battenberg, while the First Lord was the dynamic and stunningly brilliant Winston Churchill: a wonderful team for a fateful age.

This was also an age of unprecedented advance in science and engineering. Under the constant pressure of international competition and imminent war, metallurgy, ballistics, wireless telegraphy, high-explosive, marine engineering and countless other specialized trades and skills were all being developed at such a pace that the world was already entering the period of 'instant obsolescence' which we hear about today and flatter ourselves is unique to our age. The *Dreadnought* herself was obsolescent by 1914 and did not fight in the line at Jutland ten years after her spectacular debut. (Her battle cruiser contemporaries did and paid the price.)

While the Germans were more cautious and thorough in their naval development, the British tended to be more daring and enterprising, leading the way in gun bore – from 12-inch to 13.5-inch, then to 15-inch, and in 1917 to 18-inch, increasing shell weight from 850 to 3,600 pounds. This in some degree reflected British self-confidence and her offensive spirit. In any given year Britain laid down battleships which were faster and bigger and more heavily gunned than their German counterparts.

This was especially the case in 1912 when the *Warspite* was laid down at the Admiralty shipyard at Devonport, as this table comparing her with her German opposite number shows:

	displacement	main armament	speed	main hull armour
Warspite	27,500	8 x 15"	24 kts	13"
Kronprinz	25,400	10 x 12"	21 kts	14"

This does not tell the whole story. Admirable Dreadnought as the *Kronprinz* was, with her very strong defensive qualities, the broadside weight of shell of the *Warspite* was 15,600 pounds, the *Kronprinz*'s 8,600. In theory, with her superior speed and longer-ranging and more powerful guns, the British ship could shell the German ship to pieces at her chosen range without retaliation. Moreover, the *Warspite* held one further trump card. She had oil-fired boilers, her class being the first battleships in the world to be completed as all-oil burners. Economy of weight, reliability, efficiency, longer range, the ability to refuel at sea in all but heavy weather instead of a commander losing a third of his force away coaling at any given time, with the additional loss of fuel to and from base: these were some of the advantages. Coaling was inefficient, a filthy, slow and *hated* task. For oil you just plugged in and pumped! The disadvantage to Britain was the risk of her supplies being cut off. She had the most and best coal in the world; but no native oil.

The *Warspite* was the second after the *Queen Elizabeth* herself, who lent her name to the class, to be completed. The others were *Valiant*, *Barham* and *Malaya*. They were intended to form a fast battleship wing to pursue and get behind the German fleet and cut off its escape. As the 5th Battleship Squadron they formed a fast, formidable, homogeneous group unmatched in any navy, the apotheosis of the Dreadnought battleship. Bigger, faster, heavier-gunned battleships were still to come, it is true; when they did they were no longer the arbiters at sea, and the swift, steady development of the capital ship had been broken, the original principles compromised by other needs.

These splendid Queen Elizabeth ships also *looked* right: handsome, well-balanced and awe-inspiring, the cynosure of all who gazed upon them. Their record in two world wars confirmed every expectation. Although often hard pressed, only the *Barham* was sunk, struck simultaneously by three torpedoes in the Mediterranean on 25 November 1941. Only the *Warspite* demonstrated the capriciousness which so nearly proved her undoing at Jutland.

HMS *Warspite* was commissioned on 8 March 1915, Captain E. M. Philpotts. She was sorely needed by Admiral Jellicoe, C.-in-C. of the Grand Fleet, because to his dismay the *Queen Elizabeth* had been sent to the Mediterranean to support the Dardanelles operations at a time when the enemy were nearer to parity in capital ships than at any other time during the war. Her first weeks were not auspicious. First she grounded – at the high speed of 14 knots, too – in the Firth of Forth and had to go into dock for two months. Within days of joining her squadron she collided with her sister ship *Barham*, and back for more repairs she had to go. Was she an 'unlucky ship'? people were asking. Once having acquired that unhappy reputation, superstition decrees that it is almost impossible to throw it off.

However, her record at Jutland – her splendid shooting, her low casualties, her almost incredible good fortune in avoiding fatal damage from shell-fire and torpedoes alike – stopped all that. She might be unpredictable, even temperamental. But not unlucky. She carried like a talisman to the end of her days some of the honourable scars of the battering she had received.

The *Warspite* survived the enormous British naval scrapping programme ($1\frac{1}{2}$ million tons) of the end of the war and the Washington Conference of 1921–2 which drastically restricted the number and size of capital ships of the great naval powers. Instead, during the years between the wars, her profile, equipment and armament were progressively modified to meet the new needs and threats of war at sea. Her anti-aircraft guns were increased in size and number – for a while she carried a light spotter and reconnaissance aircraft on her two superimposed heavy gun turrets. Such were the short take-off runs in those days, by training the turret into wind, the machines could be flown off without power assistance from a platform extending to the gun muzzles.

In 1926 the *Warspite* emerged from the dockyard after a two-year refit with an unsightly bulge along her hull as protection against torpedo explosion, modified bridgework, and even more unsightly trunking of her two graceful funnels into one. She remained in this guise for a further decade.

Her next refit was more radical. She was gutted from stem to stern, her guns, machinery and almost all other equipment taken out. By 1937 the Royal Navy had a virtually new battleship with a single graceful funnel, a plain tower super-structure, higher-elevating, longer-ranging heavy guns, a porcupine-like display of light and heavy anti-aircraft guns, hangars for aircraft, a pole mast instead of the traditional tripod. Her protection had been greatly increased to resist the new and ever-heavier bombs and plunging shellfire which had proved so deadly at Jutland. There were now thick armoured decks over her magazines, engines and boiler rooms, the engines themselves being new lightweight geared turbines which compensated for some of the extra weight of steel. Even so her displacement was now up to nearly 32,000 tons.

When the *Warspite* emerged from dock again in March 1937 she at once revealed that no amount of face-lifting could reform her skittish character. At full speed on full helm, again her rudder jammed, sending her pirouetting as if celebrating her dangerous prank at Jutland. But this time the strains imposed on 'the old lady' as she was now called, created grave internal upsets. The new machinery had shifted, causing all sorts of trouble down in the engine rooms. Months of repairs and tests to discover and counter this failing were required before the *Warspite* was fit to take up her duties as flagship of the Mediterranean Fleet in the crisis-ridden year of 1938.

When war came in September 1939 the opening days were deceptively quiet for the *Warspite*. Italy had not yet joined in and all the action was in the Atlantic and North Sea, where German surface raiders and U-boats were active from the outset. With the destruction of a British battleship *inside* her base at Scapa Flow, the *Warspite*'s heavy guns were clearly needed nearer home, and in November 1939 she left the sun and peace of the Mediter-ranean for the cold and dangers of the Atlantic, and convoy and patrol work against a German navy equipped with the fastest and most modern ships, and supported by the greatest air force in the world.

On 10 April 1940, as the Germans swarmed into neutral Norway without warning, the *Warspite*, as flagship of Admiral Sir Charles Forbes, hastened towards the Arctic port of Narvik through which the priceless Swedish iron ore was shipped to Germany. On the same day German aircraft were sighted and began dive-bombing the battle-ship. Now at last was the testing time for her new defences. The machine-guns, eight-barrel pompoms, the Oerlikons and 5-inch dual-purpose guns filled the sky with steel and high-explosive, driving off the bombers without difficulty.

The German invasion forces had penetrated more than 100 miles into the fjord leading to Narvik with a flotilla of heavy destroyers and troop-ships, and had occupied the town. They had also laid for themselves a deadly trap. British destroyers had already taken their toll when the *Warspite* steamed up between the steep sides of the fjord, the largest warship ever to penetrate so deep into the saw-edge coastline of Norway. Above her was a spotting plane, tight-packed around her were nine destroyers. In short order this overwhelming force sank or drove ashore the eight surviving German destroyers in a rain of 15-inch, 5.5-inch and 4.7-inch shells, while the plane spotted for the gunlayers and then bombed and sank a U-boat. The thun-derous echo of shellfire against the sides of the mountains sounded a Valhalla-like overture to the *Warspite*'s new war symphony.

Later the battleship bombarded the German troops ashore. But suddenly the *Warspite* was needed back in the Mediterranean. Now that Germany had done most of the fighting in the conquest of Europe, Benito Mussolini was giving every indication of joining his crony, Adolf Hitler. And the Italian navy was a powerful force, mainly modern and equipped with battleships and especially fast 36-knot heavy cruisers. On 20 May 1940 the *Warspite* was back at Alexandria, the flagship of Admiral Sir Andrew ('ABC') Cunningham, and was about to embark on the most dangerous and prolonged series of operations of her life.

The story of sea warfare in the Mediterranean from 1940 to 1943, in which the *Warspite* took such a prominent part, is one of fluctuating fortunes, with Britain and her Empire struggling to keep open her lines of communications and supplies in an east-west direction, the Germans and Italians (the Axis powers) in a north-south direction. The crucial struggle was for Egypt, the Suez Canal, and finally for the Middle East and its oil. There were sub-plots, like the highly expensive decision to go to the aid of Greece when she was attacked. But basically it was a question of holding Egypt and Malta until at last the Allies could gather the strength to throw the Axis powers out of North Africa by advancing upon them from east and west.

Within 24 hours of Italy's declaration of war, Admiral Cunningham took his fleet to sea, his flag in the *Warspite* along with her (unmodernized) sister the *Malaya* and the old aircraft carrier *Eagle*. It was to be a sweep of the central Mediterranean to demonstrate to the Italians that this was *mare nostrum*. The enemy made no appearance either under, on, or over the sea. But this was one of the very few of *Warspite*'s operations that did not include any hostile reaction.

The fleet's next sortie like so many more in the coming months was intended to cover vital convoys from Malta to Alexandria. The Italian fleet came out in strength – two battleships and a force of heavy and light cruisers and destroyers overwhelmingly more powerful than Cunningham's. The action which followed off the coast of Calabria on 9 July 1940 looked at one time as if it might develop into a miniature Jutland. The opening rounds were similar, with the British cruisers in the van having a difficult time from well-handled Italian battleships and cruisers, and the *Warspite* coming to their rescue with well-aimed 15-inch-gun salvos. She scored an early hit on one Italian battleship, reducing her speed to 18 knots. An Italian heavy cruiser was also hit before the enemy retired at best speed behind a smokescreen. There were sporadic exchanges of fire between the light forces, but the Italian fleet like the German fleet at Jutland was concerned with escape, which it accomplished behind a skilfully laid smokescreen.

The parallel with that earlier battle ceased with the intervention of bombers from the Italian mainland. The fact that they released as many bombs on their own vessels as on the British fleet served to remind the pilots that new weapons at sea demanded new skills and responsibilities. But the passionate nature of the intercepted radio signals between the Italian fleet and the Italian bombers provided Cunningham and his men with needed light relief.

Three days later there was no humour at all in 22 separate bombing attacks each furiously pressed home. The efficiency of the *Warspite*'s anti-aircraft protection and her good luck in battle were both confirmed during this ordeal when more than 300 bombs fell around her and she was not touched once. Moreover the convoys got through safely, and that is what control of the seas is all about.

The British Mediterranean-based battleships proved their value in more direct support of the army too. On numerous occasions the navy was called upon to bombard enemy positions ashore to support an attack or a landing. A typical bombardment was that of the North African town of Bardia which the Australians were about to assault. On 3 January 1941 three of the Queen Elizabeth class of battleships, originally built to fight the Germans in another war, smashed the Italian defences of this valuable supply port. Two days later the army went in, capturing 25,000 troops.

By this time Admiral Cunningham had little to fear from the Italian battleships. On 11 November 1940 he had carried out with stunning success an operation we can now see as a miniature Pearl Harbor. From his new aircraft carrier *Illustrious* he launched at night 21 planes carrying bombs, torpedoes or flares. By dawn three Italian battleships had sunk at their moorings and Britain's maritime control of this vital area was confirmed.

A second night-action took place on 28 March 1941, this time a traditional ship-to-ship battle, although as with almost every confrontation between surface ships in every zone of operations in the Second World War, the intervention of air reconnaissance and attack, and radar, figured importantly.

A very substantial Italian fleet attempting to interfere with reinforcements to the Allied army in Greece intercepted and set about light British forces south of Crete. Admiral Cunningham rapidly put to sea, launching torpedo bombers from his carrier which located, pursued and attacked the Italian force as it fled westwards. A hit on the battle-ship *Vittorio Veneto* slowed her down, and a later torpedo attack delivered through a lethal barrage of fire crippled and brought to a standstill one of the big Italian 8-inch-gun cruisers, *Pola*. The *Warspite* with her sisters *Valiant* and *Barham* pursued the Italian force expectantly, and never was the 1911 decision to make these ultra-fast (for their time) battleships better justified. However, repair parties succeeded in raising the Italian battleship's speed again and the long pursuit continued far into the night. If the Italian admiral had not made a foolish decision to send two more of his big cruisers to the support of the crippled *Pola*, the Battle of Matapan would have been a muted and frustrating occasion for Cunningham.

But British destroyers located the Italian cruiser in the darkness and radar guided the battleships to the scene. At 10.28 pm the 15-inch fire gongs sounded out in the *Warspite* as a searchlight lit up three great shapes, and she opened fire at a mere 2,900 yards. Within a few minutes one of the briefest naval battles in history was over. The Italians were taken completely by surprise and all three heavy cruisers and two accompanying destroyers were sunk.

The year 1941 which had begun so victoriously was to become increasingly dangerous and difficult for Cunningham's fleet as German intervention in support of their failing ally manifested itself in Greece and North Africa. Just as the arrival of German generals, panzer divisions and highly efficient tanks and guns forced Britain onto the defensive on land, so the Luftwaffe's skilful pilots in planes that had helped smash the greatest army in Europe a year earlier, and U-boats brought in from the Atlantic, began to cause heavy Allied losses at sea and threatened again Admiral Cunningham's control of the Mediterranean. For long months the

Royal Navy was unable to get supplies through to the besieged and battered island of Malta, and during the evacuations from Greece and Crete the losses in lives and warships were grievous.

The *Warspite* was in the thick of the ferocious air attacks during the German invasion of Crete. The 'old lady's' luck held out with characteristic tenacity until 22 May 1941 when at 1.32 pm she was struck a savage blow by a single 250-kg bomb. It was a measure of the new rule of air power in sea warfare that a ship like the *Warspite* which had survived the full might of the German High Seas Fleet in 1916 was crippled by a tiny fighter plane, a mere midge against her 32,000 tons.

But the Luftwaffe pilot of that Messerschmitt Bf109 succeeded where Scheer and Hipper had failed, killing more of the *Warspite*'s company than those admirals' shells. The bomb struck amidships on the starboard side, penetrating an armoured deck and exploding below, starting a massive fire.

The *Warspite* escaped further injury and reached Alexandria on 24 May. After her damage had been patched up in the dockyard she departed through the Suez Canal, heading for repair in the USA and arriving at Bremerton Navy Yard, Seattle, on 11

August 1941 for a thorough repair and refit. The first and worst half of her second war was over. She had survived, as she survived Jutland, but it had been a close-run thing.

–

When the *Warspite* was taken in hand by dockyard workers the United States was enjoying an uneasy peace. When she emerged into the Pacific Ocean again in January 1942 Japanese naval air power had underlined with a bold stroke the lesson the British ship had learned in the Mediterranean, that effective sea power now depended upon effective air power. Arrogantly triumphant Japanese carrier groups were sweeping the western Pacific and the Indian Ocean. Besides the battleships at Pearl Harbor, the new British battleship *Prince of Wales* and battle cruiser *Repulse* had been sent to the bottom by airborne torpedoes and bombs, and a combined Dutch–Australian–British–American squadron had been annihilated in a surface action.

The Japanese had their eyes on the *Warspite* as she steamed west. They thought that they had got her with one-man submarines in Sydney harbour but she had already left. Avoiding carrier plane attack, which sank a carrier and two heavy cruisers not far distant, the *Warspite* arrived safely at Bombay, and later made her way home after demonstrating that even an American refit could not cure the 'old lady' of her skittishness. Even at her ripe age she enjoyed surprising her commander with a pirouette or two. And this she did while escorting a troop convoy, to the embarrassment of her crew and astonishment of those endangered.

The next time this happened the consequences were very nearly much more serious. By July 1943 the *Warspite* was back in the Mediterranean. Circumstances were very different from two years earlier. The Germans were in retreat. Italy crumbling. Early on 17 July she was ordered urgently to bombard Catania in Sicily where the 8th Army was being held up. Exact timing was imperative and the 'old lady' could make it if she steamed flat out. And so she did, with the loss of only half a knot from her original designed speed. Then her steering gremlin struck again, and she began circling, heeling hard over and almost colliding with one of her escorting vessels. By the time she had hove to and changed to emergency steering she was certain to be late. She made up for it by doing some excellent shooting even by her high standards, avoiding air and U-boat attack, and returned safely to Malta.

Two months later the *Warspite* steamed out of her base to meet the Italian fleet, not to fight it but to accept its surrender as she had met the defeated High Seas Fleet in 1918. The next day Admiral Cunningham signalled the Admiralty in London: 'The Italian battle fleet now lies at anchor under the guns of the fortress of Malta.'

In fact one of the Italian battleships was absent. The brand-new powerful *Roma* had been sent to the bottom *en route* to Malta by a new weapon of air warfare which surface ships now had to face, the radio-controlled bomb. One had sufficed to send her to her doom. And it was a similar bomb that struck the *Warspite* off Salerno on 16 September 1943, penetrating six decks and exploding deep in her bowels. The effect was devastating. All the power went out of her so that she was like a paralysed hulk.

American tugs hurried to her aid and got the 'old lady' under tow. It took three days to get her to Malta, harassed by enemy air attacks, beset by parting cables and suffering the indignity of passing through the Messina Straits broadside and out of control. Even when she arrived, listing and still helpless, in Grand Harbour, it did not seem that she could have any future. Yet, with the dogged invincibility she had shown all her fighting life and the patient determination she seemed always to inspire in her crew, she was taken first to Gibraltar and then after temporary repairs clear across the Bay of Biscay, round the north of Scotland, and back to Rosyth where she had been cheered on return from her first great battle 28 years earlier.

Nothing was going to deprive the *Warspite* of taking part in the last and most decisive battle of the war. There was no time to repair all her engines and some of her guns were still disabled, but she made it to the Normandy landings and was the first battleship to open the bombardment that cleared the coast of German batteries and allowed her sector to land safely 133,000 troops in 24 hours as a first contribution to the liberation of Europe. She fired 300 rounds on that first epochal day, returned for more ammunition, then supported American battleships in their sector when their ammunition ran low. In the end she wore out her guns and had to proceed north to Rosyth again to have them replaced. On the way she struck a mine, and at once went into one of her gyrations. This time it was not an old lady's whim. Her hull, still only temporarily patched from that ferocious explosion off Salerno, was gravely damaged again and she lay for long dead on the ocean.

Once more and for the last time she was patched up. Her guns were still sorely needed and so long as she could float and move through the water and fire her guns, that was all that was asked of her. Bombardment duty was a long way from cutting through the water at full speed to fire broadsides at the German fleet in 1916. But the nature of sea warfare had changed fundamentally in her own lifetime. So, by 25 August 1944 she was off Brest again, supporting American troops. Later she crawled up-Channel and on 3 November her guns fired in anger for the last time at enemy batteries at the mouth of the River Scheldt.

And now at last, in her thirtieth year, the 'old lady's' time was up, and she was moved to the Reserve Fleet. In April 1947 she left Spithead under tow for the Clyde for breaking up. The *Warspite* was having none of that humiliation, however, and when her tow parted in heavy weather she drifted ashore, coming to rest on the rocks in the appropriately noble setting of a Cornish bay. A tough old Dreadnought to the last, it took them until 1956 to complete the dismemberment of one of the Royal Navy's greatest men o'war.

Java

Light cruiser, 1925, Netherlands

The Royal Netherlands Navy of the twentieth century bore little relation in size and influence to the powerful force which challenged England and Spain 300 years earlier. But the Dutch were no less a maritime race and the 12,000 personnel who manned the small force of cruisers, destroyers, torpedo boats and submarines in 1940 were as efficient and keen as in those distant days of De Ruyter and the *Zeven Provincien*. The greater part of this small navy's responsibility was still very much the same, namely the protection of possessions in the Far East, which had been under Dutch rule since that nation had broken up the Portuguese trading monopoly early in the seventeenth century.

Most of the Royal Netherlands Navy was not involved in the German invasion of Holland in May

1940 and was therefore available for the protection of Java, Sumatra, Borneo and other Dutch possessions which became increasingly threatened by Japan after the German conquest of the homeland. One of the warships of this tight, homogeneous force was the *Java*, a typical and thoroughly satisfactory example of light cruiser construction. She was laid down at Flushing in the month Jutland was fought and when Holland was in neutral isolation on the borders of an embattled Germany. She was, in fact, of German design, powered by German machinery, and armed with Swedish guns. As she fought alongside the Australians, British and Americans, and against Japan, she could claim internationalism as well as heroism in her last battle.

The German design was evident in the *Java*'s Teutonic profile and she was in every way an impressive-looking vessel, with a top speed of over 30 knots and a main armament of 10 x 5.9-inch guns. Before the Second World War broke out she had a thorough refit and modernization, and when she emerged in 1935 her much increased anti-aircraft armament and the two seaplanes she carried acknowledged the new influence of air power upon the world's navies.

After the opening of hostilities in the Pacific with the Japanese attack on Pearl Harbor on 7 December 1941, and the inevitable involvement of Australia, New Zealand, Britain and Holland, the Japanese tide marched implacably across the East – from the Malaysian peninsula to New Guinea, from the Aleutians to the Philippines. There was little to slow its pace. The American battleship fleet and the British Force Z of two more capital ships based on Singapore were all crippled or sunk in the first days, and the rule of constitutional democracy appeared to be as swiftly doomed in the East as it had been largely destroyed in the West a year earlier.

The rich Dutch islands were among the first to face attack, and by the end of January the defences of Borneo had been broken and it was clear that Sumatra and Java were next in line for invasion. Through the appalling weeks of the turn of the year, makeshift defences were engineered under all the difficulties of different languages, practices and armaments. The gravest weakness was in air power. The Allies had almost nothing, and the few planes were outdated. The Japanese had demonstrated to the world the superior numbers, equipment and personnel of their naval air arm, and for this reason alone the final outcome was in little doubt.

On the naval side the Allies had succeeded in cobbling together a force of light and heavy cruisers and destroyers which on paper was quite formidable. But it lacked homogeneity, experience of working together, and above all air support. By mid-February 1942 the ships had been on almost constant operations and often under air attack for two months, the crews were weary, and the overall spirit was not optimistic.

The force that gathered at Soerabaya on the north Java coast consisted of the following ships:

	tons	armament	speed		
Exeter	8,400	6 x 8"	32	British	1929
Houston	9,000	9* x 8"	33	USA	1929
De Ruyter	6,500	7 x 5.9"	32	Dutch	1935
Java	6,600	10 x 5.9"	31	Dutch	1921
Perth	7,000	8 x 6"	32	Australian	1934

Destroyers: 5 American
3 British
3 Dutch

* 3 disabled

The Japanese attacking force consisted of four battleships, four carriers, backed by heavy and light cruisers and destroyers, of which the following were actually engaged with the Allies on 27 February 1942:

	tons	armament	speed	
Nachi	10,000	10 x 8"	33	1927
Haguro	10,000	10 x 8"	33	1928
Naka	5,200	7 x 5.5"	33	1925
Jintsu	5,200	7 x 5.5"	33	1923

Destroyers: 14

These figures take no account of the great superiority of Japanese torpedoes, something which took the American and Allied navies by surprise. The pressures of an earlier war had led the British navy to investigate a new and more effective propellant for torpedoes than compressed air, which restricted their range and speed and left a warning trail which often allowed the target to take evasive action. Oxygen fuel was the alternative most favoured by the British, and early experiments showed its considerably greater power. It also proved to be highly volatile and dangerous to handle, and the decision was made to cease experiments for safety reasons. The Japanese, however, were happy to accept the technical information on oxygen propulsion from the British under the treaty between the two countries, as they had the advanced knowledge of the Royal Navy on naval air experience, which included priceless knowledge on torpedo-carrying aircraft and carrier take-off and landing procedures.

All this was carefully tucked away in the Japanese files, and when rearmament gained momentum again in the late 1920s, a programme of renewed experiment into the development of an entirely new form of torpedo was put in hand. The result was the 'Long Lance', a brilliant technical achievement but a weapon that could be almost as dangerous to handle as it was destructive of the enemy. Many men had died in its development; now many more were to succumb to its devastating power. The Long Lance Japanese oxygen-powered torpedo in 1941 had a range of 22 sea miles and a speed at shorter range of 49 knots. Its explosive warhead had the unprecedented destructive power of 1,200 pounds. The Long Lance made all compressed air and steam-driven torpedoes obsolete, as the shell had earlier outdated the cannon ball. The Japanese force that was to meet the Dutch Admiral Doorman had them in great numbers.

Rear-Admiral Karel Doorman was appointed commander of the 'Combined Striking Force' on a point of courtesy. The senior American commander was Captain A. H. Rooks USN, the senior British officer Captain O. L. Gordon RN of the *Exeter*, and the *Java* was in the able hands of Captain P. B. M. Straelen RNN. In order to simplify communications and signalling a Dutch-speaking American liaison officer was on board the Dutch flagship to translate and transmit to the English-speaking ships the Admiral's directions.

Most of the vessels had been more or less damaged in earlier operations by the skill and ferocity of Japanese air attacks. The American cruiser, for example, had been blooded on 4 February by a heavy bomb on her main deck aft, which knocked out the triple 8-inch gun turret and burned to death some 50 of her crew.

Almost as soon as Admiral Doorman had assembled his force at Soerabaya an invasion convoy was reported closing on the island 190 miles to the north-east. He took his ships to sea without delay, searched for 24 hours – experiencing a fierce bombing attack at dawn – and returned in order to top up his destroyers' fuel. Before he could drop anchor further convoys escorted by naval forces were reported to the north, and the ships again reversed course and made for the nearest force which was reported to be only some 75 miles away.

The cruisers were formed up in line ahead, the flagship *De Ruyter* in the lead followed by the two 8-inch-gun cruisers, the *Perth* and the *Java* taking up the rear. The British destroyers acted as a forward screen, the Dutch and American destroyers taking station to port and at the rear. Speed was 20 knots, course 315° – and they had not got a plane between them. Doorman signalled urgently for some sort of air support, recalling the recent fate of so many ships more powerful than his own which had been sunk in the past weeks because of lack of air cover. Air command ashore decided that the handful of slow and obsolescent fighters available should escort the few remaining dive-bombers in an attempt to destroy Japanese troop transports instead. As if to underline this inadequacy three Japanese scouting planes were sighted on the northern horizon. The Combined Striking Force steamed on fatefully towards their miniature Battle of Tsu-Shima which was so soon to be played out to its disastrous conclusion.

The British destroyer *Electra*, which 11 weeks earlier had witnessed the destruction of the mighty *Prince of Wales* and *Repulse* at the hands of the Japanese navy air arm, sighted masts on the horizon. These were later identified as belonging to a cruiser and destroyers steaming across their bows, just as Togo had crossed Rozhestvensky's 'T'. The dark shapes of more enemy ships rose up on the skyline. Doorman ordered 26 knots from his cruisers, and as the American official historian reported, 'Perth ran up her big white battle ensigns on the fore and main, and to old-timers on board Houston the "meteor flag of England" looked good'.

The first sparkle of Japanese gun flashes sprang out at 4.14 pm at 28,000 yards, and even at this extreme range for 8-inch guns it was accurate shooting. For seven minutes the Allied ships were unable to reply. Then, to prevent his 'T' being crossed, Doorman ordered a 20° turn to port, bringing the two lines on an approximately westerly course but still at too great a range for the guns of the *Java* and the other two smaller cruisers to open fire. Doorman had previously shown hesitancy in his command and this failure to close and allow superiority in the smaller calibres to take effect was at variance with the conduct of the admiral after whom his ship was named, and of his own commanders.

The flagship was the first to receive a hit, at 4.31 pm, although all the allied cruisers had been straddled time and again. The 8-inch shell pierced to the engine room but failed to explode and the *De Ruyter* steamed on, still defenceless, through the forest of waterspouts. Now the Japanese light cruisers and destroyers added their weight to the attack, turning in at maximum speed to launch their Long Lances and then steaming between the lines to lay a smokescreen. Again luck was with the Allied squadron. Not one of the ships was hit, and the *Perth* hit and crippled one of the Japanese destroyers. The purpose of the screen was to conceal themselves from Allied gunfire. At the same time they continued to fire, their shots being spotted by the seaplanes hovering like vultures above the scene of battle.

After little more than an hour this gun duel reached its turning point when the Japanese shooting was at last rewarded. An 8-inch shell plunged from great range onto the *Exeter*, tore through her deck armour and exploded in the engine room. The British cruiser, hero of the fight with the *Graf Spee* early in the war, rapidly lost speed and brought the battle line into confusion. The *Houston* was forced to turn sharply to port to avoid the *Exeter*, and the *Perth* and *Java* followed in the belief that they had failed to see the signal for a turn, thus leaving the flagship to steam on alone for a while. A few minutes later one of the Dutch destroyers was hit by a Long Lance, exploded, broke in two and sank almost at once, demonstrating again to the shocked eyewitnesses the mysterious power of Japanese torpedoes.

Doorman ordered his cruisers to turn to port away from the enemy and attempted to reform his line. It was at this moment that the lack of liaison and practice together revealed itself most disastrously. In the failing light, and through the drifting smoke from the battle, the screen, and the burning *Exeter*, signals went unseen or were misunderstood.

The *Java* at this stage was only catching glimpses of the enemy but was getting in salvoes of 6-inch fire to some effect, and watched the destroyers go bravely in towards the enemy in compliance with a desperate order from the admiral. These scattered destroyers succeeded in keeping the Japanese light forces from getting near the crippled *Exeter* but took heavy punishment themselves. The little *Electra* hit the *Jintsu* before being forced to a halt with a shell in her engine room. She fought on valiantly but was pounded to pieces and sank at about 6 pm.

Half an hour earlier the *Java* succeeded in joining forces with the remaining cruisers and followed Doorman on a south-easterly course in an effort to intercept the troop transports before they could get their men ashore. *Exeter* was endeavouring to make Soerabaya at 15 knots, escorted by a destroyer, and succeeded in getting off a few rounds when she obtained intermittent sightings of the enemy.

In the early hours of the night, while Doorman led the *Houston*, *Perth* and *Java* in a vain and blind attempt to locate the transports, the enemy watched their every move. The Japanese might not have radar (a department in which they lagged seriously behind) but they were supremely skilful in night fighting. Working in relays, ubiquitous spotter seaplanes hovered over Doorman's force, dropping flares from time to time to reveal their position to the cruisers and destroyers, at the same time exasperating the helpless Allied commanders.

For the *Java* the end of the battle came as swiftly as the opening had been slow to develop. After engaging in a brief and ineffectual gun duel with the two Japanese heavy cruisers by the light of flares and starshells, the Dutch cruiser was struck by a Long Lance at 11.20 pm. The tremendous explosion immediately brought the ship to a standstill. Briefly she lay wrecked and blazing, her fires lighting up the sea far about her. Then she sank, going down close to the island after which she was named and which she had bravely defended for seven hours.

Her flagship, similarly struck, went down a few minutes before her. Doorman just had time to get off a signal to the two surviving cruisers ordering them to retire to Batavia at once, thus depriving himself and his ships' companies of any chance of rescue.

The reprieve for the remainder of Doorman's force was tragically brief. The *Houston* and *Perth* attempted to slip through the Sunda Strait the following night but met a further invasion force that was even more heavily escorted. They struck back hard and valiantly but nothing could save them against such odds, and again the Long Lances gave the *coup de grâce*. The crippled *Exeter* and her escort followed the same course, and met the same fate, a few hours later.

With the destruction of the optimistically titled Combined Striking Force there was nothing to delay the invasion of Java, a fact which the Japanese exploited with their customary efficiency. Although the Battle of the Java Sea was an overwhelming Japanese victory, the sacrifice of the *Java* and the other cruisers was not entirely in vain. There were numerous lessons to be learned from the battle. The Long Lances had certainly shown themselves as deadly weapons. But the Japanese were improvident and inaccurate with them, in one attack alone firing 43 without making a hit. There was a high failure rate with the Japanese shells, too. The enemy's most effective skill was in the air–sea cooperation, a consequence of the rigorous training of Admiral Isoroku Yamamoto, the officer who was as much the father of the Japanese air arm as Togo was father of the navy itself.

Saratoga

Aircraft carrier, 1927, USA

In July 1910 a British pioneer pilot Mr Claude Grahame-White flew his biplane over the British fleet anchored off the Cornish coast. The flight 'caused much reflection as to the effect of these machines on our Dreadnought policy'. This was pure journalese, like the cartoon in the New York *World* showing Wright stringbags dive-bombing a fleet at sea. In November of the same year an American flyer Eugene Ely took off from a platform rigged over the stern of the cruiser *Birmingham*. These events were good copy for a brief mention in the newspapers and were then forgotten by the public. At a period of increasing tension between the European powers service chiefs could not afford to ignore the airplane. In Britain both the First Lord of the Admiralty and the First Sea Lord,

Admiral Prince Louis of Battenberg, encouraged experiments and the formation of a naval air arm. A year after Ely's flight, Lieutenant C. R. Samson RN flew a plane off a platform on a battleship, and a few weeks later the Secretary of the Committee of Imperial Defence, Rear-Admiral Sir Charles Ottley, in a letter to Prince Louis, wrote:

> I gather from private conversation with [Samson] and his colleagues that they anticipate that in a very short time the aeroplane may have developed suffi-ciently for practical use with a fleet...

The 'practical use' related at this stage to little more than scouting service. An appreciation of its destructive potential was still some time away, although not all that distant. Under the press of war the British advanced rapidly in the development of naval aviation with both heavier- and lighter-than-air machines. Scouting planes were accommodated on the turrets of battleships and took off from dizzily short platforms, or even more hazardously from towed rafts. In 1914 the Royal Navy commissioned its first aircraft carrier but her planes could only take off, not land. In 1917 the Royal Navy ordered the first take-off-land-on carrier and by then was operating torpedo bombers with the fleet – the first 'tin fish' having been dropped by a Short Seaplane in the Solent on 28 July 1914. The seaplane carrier *Engadine* launched a wireless-equipped scouting seaplane at the Battle of Jutland. It transmitted important news, too, but no one took any notice.

The Japanese learned the lessons of air power early, laid down a carrier and introduced British machines and techniques. It was all part of her immense programme of naval rearmament in competition with the USA which was temporarily halted by the Washington Naval Conference of 1921–2. By this time the British, Japanese and Americans all had programmes under way for the construction of leviathan super-Dreadnoughts. These were all to be over 35,000 tons and one design discussed by the American Bureau of Construction called for 80,000 tons and 15 x 18-inch guns. Clearly this insanity could only lead to international bankruptcy.

Most of these monsters never got beyond the drawing board. A number were started but only one, the British *Hood*, was completed as designed, the biggest fighting ship in the world for two decades. Under the terms of the Treaty, the Japanese and Americans were each permitted to complete two of theirs on the stocks as giant aircraft carriers. In 1942 the Japanese lost both of theirs at the Battle of Midway. The Americans lost one of theirs early in the Pacific war. Only the USS *Saratoga* survived the Second World War as a reminder of those phantom fleets dreamed up in the aftermath of the bloodiest war in history. In her origin, history and war record she must be counted as the greatest carrier in the brief history of naval aviation.

-

The United States Navy tended to follow Tirpitz's German principles of heavy ship construction, which placed a higher priority on protection than speed. From the beginning American Dreadnoughts were built with immense strength and thickness of armour plate, with up to 18 inches on the turrets and 14-inch side armour belts. For the Dreadnought's first decade – 1906–16 – the USA built no battle cruisers, believing they had no useful part to play in a two-ocean navy. But doubts began to set in after this type seemed to prove its worth early in the European war, and in February 1916 the president of the Naval War College told the Senate Naval Committee that no more battleships should be laid down until the navy had at least two divisions of battle cruisers.

The designs that stemmed from this resolution were the most radical – not to say bizarre – since the *Dreadnought* herself. The ships were to be of 35,000 tons, mount 10 x 14-inch guns and be able to steam at the unprecedented speed of 35 knots. In order to attain this speed the greater part of their hulls would be given up to space for boiler rooms, engines and fuel, and as there was little provision for armour the ships were going to be even more vulnerable than some of Fisher's latest battle cruiser excesses which mounted 18-inch guns.

This design got a frosty reception from outside the navy; and then Jutland was fought, with its toll of four battle cruisers and the crippling of others, and no Dreadnought battleship losses. This outcome seemed to reinforce the fears of the critics, and it was not until 1919 that revised designs were completed for much tougher battle cruisers, like Germany's latest, the *Hindenburg*.

Six of these battle cruisers were laid down 1920–1, bearing honoured names in American history – *Lexington*, *Ranger*, *United States*, *Constitution*, *Constellation* and *Saratoga*. They were hardly less extreme than the preliminary draft designs and provided for 8 x 16-inch armament, 35 knots and 43,500 tons, the greater displacement being largely accounted for by the improved protection. Today, war games enthusiasts no doubt enjoy mythical Pacific battles with these massive battle cruisers and the six battleships that were also planned, against their equally awesome Japanese counterparts.

Then, with the ink not yet dry on the Washington Treaty, all construction was scrapped, except on the *Lexington* and *Saratoga*, which were limited by the Treaty to 33,000 tons. This was achieved by shedding the heavy guns, their turrets and barbettes, and radically reducing deck and side armour plate.

The metamorphosis of the *Saratoga* demanded great ingenuity and occupied almost five years. The final configuration signalled a new unlovely era in fighting ship appearance, and the end of the graceful and balanced Dreadnought, just as the hideous ironclad had replaced the splendid three-decker ship-of-the-line.

But when the *Saratoga* launched her squadrons of high-level and dive bombers, her torpedo planes and fighters, even the layman could see that once again fighting effectiveness had taken on a new dimension and the increase in 'firepower' of a squadron of bombers over 16-inch guns was as immense as the shell gun's had once been over the cannon.

The *Saratoga* was a great slab of a ship, a slab of an island superstructure and a huge slab of a single funnel stuck on a slab of hull 888 feet long. The British converted three of their battle cruisers into carriers, too, but they were much smaller than the *Saratoga* whose vast flight deck was a dream of spaciousness in the eyes of any pilot – including the first ever to land on her, Mark A. Mitscher, the future notable admiral.

She was not only the largest but the fastest carrier in the world by a wide margin, showing 34 knots with ease. She was also the heaviest armed, with 8 x 8-inch guns and the usual modest scattering of lighter, high-angle guns considered adequate in 1928. With her sister she was the wonder ship as well as the ugly duckling of the US Navy, distinctive at the longest range, and, especially at high speed, as formidable a sight as any battleship. America might still be without a battle cruiser – and probably none the worse for that – but she now had a pair of new Dreadnoughts of the air age whose 'guns' could reach as far as the range of her bombers.

In March 1938 during one of the numerous 'Fleet Problem' exercises in which the *Saratoga* engaged until real war began, the carrier secretly approached to within 100 miles of Pearl Harbor where she launched her planes. The 'attack' took the defenders completely by surprise. Three years later it seemed that the lesson had still not been learned, although the base was by then equipped with radar. Providentially the *Saratoga*, like all the navy's precious carriers, was absent from Pearl Harbor when planes from Japanese converted ex-battle cruisers swept in on the island at dawn 7 December 1941.

From the explosion of the first bomb on the first American battleship to be damaged, the Japanese war of 1941–5 was a carrier war. New battleships and modernized older battleships played a vital role in bombardment and escort capacities *so long as the sky above them was not controlled by the enemy*. But the outcome of every Japanese attack, every American counter-attack, every clash of the fleets, every landing on every island, was governed by the plane, based either on airstrips or more often the rolling decks of carriers. At one time, in the darkest days of the Pacific war for America, she was down to just two serviceable carriers. So prodigious was American industrial capacity that she was later operating almost one hundred.

The *Saratoga* was at San Diego at the time of Pearl Harbor, and hastened to give support to the wrecked Pacific Fleet with a number of Marine Corps aircraft in her hangars destined for the important base at Wake Island. Eight days after the Japanese attack the big carrier steamed into the litter and carnage of Pearl Harbor to refuel. Wake Island fell before she could carry out her task. The triumphant Japanese carriers were ranging unchecked over the Pacific and later the Indian Ocean, too. Nothing, it seemed, could deter them. The *Lexington* was lost at the Coral Sea engagement and the *Saratoga* herself was gravely damaged by a Japanese torpedo on 11 January and had to limp back to Pearl Harbor for emergency repairs.

At Bremerton Navy Yard the carrier was repaired permanently and at the same time her anti-aircraft armament was greatly augmented and modernized. Her 8-inch battery, useless in this new air warfare, had already been removed.

The Pacific War began seriously for the *Saratoga* in July 1942 when she took a leading part in the opening of the Guadalcanal campaign. The Japanese had at last been checked at Midway when no fewer than four of her best carriers had been sunk. Their loss and the loss of all their aircraft was less serious than the deaths of the air crews. Japan had built up an unsurpassed body of skilful and utterly dedicated air crews to man her first-class naval air fleets. But their decimation after the early almost unopposed Japanese advances was in the end to prove fatal.

By July American self-confidence had been partly restored and there was a determination to switch to the offensive. The first target was the Solomon Islands in the south-west Pacific, specifically the island of Guadalcanal where the Japanese forces were consolidating their invasion and preparing an airfield.

On 16 July the *Saratoga*, as Task Force flagship, acted as host at a hastily convened conference at sea south of Fiji. The Task Force Commander, Vice-Admiral Frank Fletcher, one of the founders of victory at Midway, had only 48 hours to brief his officers, including Australians, and coordinate duties among them. Throughout the Pacific War the spectre of the early disaster at the Battle of the Java Sea hung over all considerations of multi-national operations. The Americans always preferred to fight alone. But speed, followed by secrecy, were the two first priorities of this Guadalcanal operation.

On 6 August 1942 the enormous amphibious task force, the first of so many in the three-year-long struggle that lay ahead, approached the entrance to Indispensable Strait between Guadalcanal and Malaita. Besides the *Saratoga*, Fletcher had two newer but smaller carriers, the *Enterprise* and *Wasp*, supported by the big guns of the modern battleship *North Carolina*, six cruisers and 16 destroyers.

Thanks to poor weather and visibility, the landing by US Marines took the Japanese completely by surprise, and in a short time the airfield was in American hands. The moment the weather cleared the Japanese reacted violently and a heavy force of escorted twin-engine bombers and dive-bombers swarmed over the vulnerable landing ships. The *Saratoga* launched her Hellcat fighters which joined the furious dogfight with Japanese Zeros and bombers.

The true meaning of naval airpower in this new age of sea warfare could be clearly defined at the end of the day's fighting. Fourteen Japanese bombers and some of the escorting Zeros had been shot down, and not one of the vital American transports had been touched. It was the same story the next day when the Japanese sent in torpedo and dive-bombers. In the past when their rule of the skies was unchallenged the Japanese had struck with terrible effect and almost no casualties, wrecking the battle-ship fleet at Pearl Harbor, sinking the British capital ships *Prince of Wales* and *Repulse* in the South China Sea three days later, the British heavy cruisers *Corn-wall* and *Dorsetshire*, the first-ever carrier *Hermes* on 9 April off Ceylon, and numerous smaller ships.

Faced by squadrons of Wildcat fighters it was a different story. The Japanese machines were shot out of the sky and only one torpedo found its target, and that not fatally. No exhibition could demonstrate more clearly that now control of the sea depended on control of the sky.

When Admiral Fletcher misguidedly withdrew his carriers from the heat of the action to a refuelling rendezvous the tide of the battle at once turned in the favour of the Japanese. They sent in their heavy and light cruisers at night to tear apart the protecting Allied cruiser and destroyer force in what came to be known as the Battle of Savo Sea. The Japanese force could and should have been slaughtered during its withdrawal. But there was not a carrier within range.

During the last week in August carrier warfare flared up to a climax of mutual destruction off Guadalcanal. The first prize was the airfield, that static and indestructible carrier. Much of the fighting was preceded by games of half-blind man's buff, the Japanese relying on their scout planes to keep track of the American carriers' movements, the Americans relying (too heavily) on their radar.

The only guns that fired were anti-aircraft, both sides being able to fill the sky with a seemingly impenetrable screen of high-explosive. Tactics were based on the range of aircraft, speed of launching and on having the right machines refuelled and in the air at the right time. The Japanese had lost heavily at Midway through having machines refuelling on deck when the American dive-bombers came down. Luck played its part, too. And for the first time since the days of sail, wind was an important consideration: turning the *Saratoga* into wind every time she launched or landed an aircraft being a time-consuming business.

First blood went to the *Saratoga*. On the morning of 24 August Japanese scout planes were sighted on several occasions. Each was shot down in turn by the carrier's fighters. But the American radar revealed a blip that could have been the main Japanese carrier force. Admiral Fletcher, hopeful that he might be at the start of an engagement as victorious as Midway, launched an attack from the long flight deck of his biggest carrier. Thirty dive-bombers and eight torpedo planes roared off the *Saratoga* and formed up to head towards the suspected Japanese force.

The bombers failed to find the main target. But it was not to be a fruitless mission. They sighted the long cigar-like shape of the carrier *Ryujo* right below and at once turned over on their backs and screamed down through the multiple puffs of heavy anti-aircraft fire. Hits were made with 1,000-pound bombs, and then the torpedo planes went in to finish her off. Not a single plane was lost, and there were great celebrations onboard the *Saratoga* that evening.

Eight days later the *Saratoga* took her second torpedo hit, and she lay dead in the water for anxious hours while repair squads fought to bring life back to her engines. She flew off her planes and was taken in tow by the cruiser *Minneapolis*. It was November 1942 before she was ready for action again.

The next twelve months were to be the most active of her life. Steaming in company for much of the time with the British carrier *Victorious* and the USS *Princeton*, she operated off the Eastern Solomons and took a leading part in the invasion of Bougainville. Raids on Rabaul to protect the invading forces led to massive destruction of Japanese shipping. Later in the commission she was engaged in the furious fighting for Makin and Tarawa in the Gilbert Islands.

In desperate need of an overhaul, the *Saratoga* steamed to Pearl Harbor again on 7 January 1944 where she was fitted with even heavier anti-aircraft defences. After a further brief period of fighting in the Marshall Islands area, the *Saratoga* was detached first to Australia and then to Ceylon to impart the experience of Pacific air fighting to the aircrews of the newly-arrived British carrier *Illustrious*, following this with a live demonstration over Soerabaja in Java. Later the carrier continued its training role at Pearl Harbor where she worked up an air group specifically intended for night fighting. The exceptionally large area of her flight deck made her especially suitable for night work.

The *Saratoga*'s last tour of duty was in the area of the Japanese home islands, and her newly-trained night fighter pilots saw action patrolling Iwo Jima in the dark. So far in her more than three years of service, often in the heat of the fighting, the *Saratoga* had escaped damage from the air, though there was no plumper target in the Pacific. Her luck could not last for ever, and it broke at last on 21 February 1945 when a strong force of Japanese bombers broke through the carrier's defences and scored six bomb hits.

The damage was appalling. Fires broke out in the hangars, her deck forward was shattered, 123 of her crew were dead and many more injured. The firefighting crews struggled to save the ship and at length got the fires under control. Again 'the fighting lady' struggled back to the west coast and was repaired at Bremerton Navy Yard. But her future role was a pacific one, that of bringing home thousands of American naval veterans after the surrender of Japan, almost 30,000 in all.

The *Saratoga*'s war record was unsurpassed. She had fought in many of the toughest campaigns and had during her lifetime of $17\frac{1}{2}$ years logged over 98,000 landings. The big bluff ship deserved a less humiliating end than she suffered. Having survived so many Japanese bomb attacks, it was hard on the old girl that she should be sunk by an American bomb – an atomic bomb at that – at the Bikini Atoll test. Just to show the stuff she was made of she shrugged off the first blast. But a second underwater explosion a mere 500 yards away sent her to the bottom.

Kelly

Destroyer, 1939, Britain

The combined science and art of naval architecture has throughout history been applied as sharply to the smaller fighting ships as to the largest. In many respects the skill of the shipwright and naval constructor has been tested more keenly on the small, fast ship, in which any miscalculation in stability, machinery power output or hull configuration is more sensitively responded to than in a great ship-of-the-line or 30,000-ton Dreadnought. The skill of the master shipwright was more wonderfully exercised on the swift and beautiful frigates of France, Holland, Spain, Britain and then the United States at the turn of the eighteenth and nineteenth centuries than on any contemporary three-decker.

Those exquisite jewels of the Napoleonic and Revolutionary wars and the Anglo-American war of 1812, like the USS *President*,[5] with a rig including skysails, were superseded at length by steel cruisers of various classes, all hideous to the modern eye, with various mixed armaments and coal-fired boilers and reciprocating engines giving speeds of around 18–20 knots.

Grace and proportion were revived in naval architecture in the smallest class of all, the cutter of the late nineteenth century – the torpedo boat. The torpedo boat began life as a diminutive, wet little boat displacing around 100 tons, carrying a single, short-range torpedo and operating only in coastal waters. Even smaller boats were carried on the decks of ironclads, precursors of the torpedo-carrying, ship-borne planes from 1917.

By the mid-1890s the 125-ton 25-knot torpedo boat was commonplace, armed with a pair of 18-inch torpedoes and perhaps a 3-pounder gun or two. Life onboard was tough and restricted, earning hard-lying money for the crew. These boats were able to steam with the fleet although their range was severely limited.

Admiral Fisher, midwife to the later Dreadnought and battle cruiser, countered French fleet torpedo boats in 1893 with 'Torpedo Boat Catchers', later called Torpedo Boat Destroyers, soon abridged to Destroyers. Fisher called for a speed of 27 knots and powerful gun armament as well as torpedo armament.

The battle fleet's counter-measures against the destroyer increased with its increase in size and the range and speed of the torpedoes. A typical First World War destroyer topped 1,000 tons in displacement, carried guns of up to 4-inch calibre and could steam over 30 knots. They were used in numbers in their primary defensive and offensive roles with the fleet and also in convoy and anti-U-boat work. The Royal Navy's appetite for them was as insatiable as Nelson's for frigates. In North Sea actions, notably at Jutland, the sight of massed flotillas of destroyers going into the attack was in its own way quite as awe-inspiring as the main action of the Dreadnoughts themselves.

As in so many other departments of *matériel* the destroyer advanced very little after the conclusion of 'the war to end wars'. A representative American destroyer of the early 1930s might displace

1,400 tons, carry an armament of 5 x 5-inch guns and eight torpedo tubes and possess a maximum speed of around 36 knots. The destroyer's main role in the American, British and Japanese navies was still to work with the fleet in line-of-battle actions between heavy ships. The threat of the bomber and torpedo-carrying plane had influenced design and fleet tactics very little in the British and US navies; rather more in the Japanese navy.

The triple threat to the free democracies from Germany, Italy and Japan during the later 1930s resulted in rapid rearmament and new conceptions of design in all classes of fighting ship, not least the destroyer. As war again became imminent the Germans, Americans and Japanese constructed big heavy-hitting destroyers that were as formidable as First World War light cruisers. Italian destroyers, as beautiful as Renaissance sculptures, could make 45 knots.

The British contribution to the revival of destroyer construction was seen first in the Tribal class and then the 'J' and 'K' classes. Between them these highly successful vessels marked both a turning point and final culmination in the design of destroyers. All that influenced subsequent destroyer design stemmed from them. The Tribals were designed to answer the much bigger and more heavily gunned destroyers being built abroad with the emphasis on gunpower (8 x 4.7-inch) rather than torpedo power (a single set of four tubes), and a displacement of close on 2,000 tons. They subsequently did good service, notably in the Norwegian campaign, but in the next design there was a reaction and a greater emphasis on the torpedo, less on the gun, and a considerable reduction in size.

The 'J's and 'K's, of which the *Kelly* was to become the most famous, were the result of urgent design discussion carried out in 1936, a year of increasing international tension and threat of war.

The man responsible for destroyer design in the Royal Navy at this time was the naval constructor A. P. Cole. Cole was not an easy man to work with but possessed a brilliant and radical mind. Captain Lord Louis Mountbatten also contributed directly to the design of the ship he was subsequently to make famous.

Lord Mountbatten joined the Royal Navy as a cadet at Osborne in 1913 as Prince Louis Francis of Battenberg. His father, the husband of Queen

Victoria's favourite grand-daughter, had then been a naval officer for 45 years and had reached the top as First Sea Lord. Because of violent anti-German feeling the family had been obliged to change their name to Mountbatten. At the age of 33 in the spring of 1934 Commander Lord Louis Mountbatten was captain of the destroyer *Daring* in the Mediterranean Fleet. While his ship was in dry dock he decided to make life more comfortable for himself, something he has never neglected to do when the opportunity occurred. It was no more than having hot and cold running water fitted into his cabin, and this was being carried out by Maltese dockyard workers when Cole came onboard to investigate, discovering a hole apparently being made in the destroyer's bottom. He reported this scandal to the Admiral ashore, without reference to Lord Louis, who was then summoned to the Admiral's office in order that Cole might repeat the charge in front of him.

The young commander denied that he was sabotaging his ship, explained that all he wanted to do was to tap one of the outlet pipes for the waste water from his basin and expressed surprise that a civilian should be snooping round his ship without permission. Cole was ordered to apologize, and Lord Louis, who had long before recognized the man's genius, saw to it that they now became friends and allies in the design of new destroyer construction.

The team worked very well. Lord Louis, with his powerful social and service influence, caused Cole's more radical and more controversial ideas to get through the red tape and reactionary opposition. For example, Cole wanted two boilers only in his new design, each giving 20,000 horsepower, or in total about the same as the battle cruiser *Invincible* (31 boilers), a testament to the progress of boiler design in 30 years. The Naval Staff insisted on three. There had never been fewer. It was dangerous to rely on two, and so on. Lord Louis worked on the Controller of the Navy, Admiral Sir Reginald Henderson, conveniently a neighbour in Sussex, and eventually got his way.

The consequence of this victory was that the *Kelly* had only one funnel, with all the advantage of improved visibility and simplicity and the saving of space above as well as below, where the two boilers were tucked back to back against the funnel up-take; and the additional advantage of cruising faster and more economically on one boiler.

The naval constructor and the naval commander worked closely on other aspects of the design, including most importantly the adoption of longitudinal framing for the construction of the ship's hull, a system long used in heavy ship construction. In essence it gave greater emphasis to the lengthwise girders in the framework of the ship's hull and fewer but stouter transverse frames. This system, Cole believed, would provide a destroyer with a stronger and more resilient hull to meet the buffets of service, both from natural and explosive causes.

The *Kelly* and her consorts also enjoyed much improved accommodation for the ship's company, with spacious mess decks and – wonder of wonders! – bathrooms. No hard-lying money to be had here. There was even a proper little cinema store to stow the portable projector safely abaft the funnel. Mountbatten's concern for comfort was not a hedonistic exercise. He believed that a sailor worked more efficiently if he was not cramped, frozen or soaked. For this reason he devised a part-covered bridge, precursor to the all-enclosed bridge which eventually superseded the all-exposed bridges of earlier destroyers. It had been accepted as a normal condition in destroyer service that bridge personnel were more or less permanently soaked in all but the most placid seas. Seaboots, oilskins, frozen eyebrows in northern waters – all this was part of the cherished life-style of the small boat sailor. Mountbatten saw it differently. His destroyer service told him that he would be at a disadvantage in action under average conditions on his bridge.

The Mountbatten bridge, devised in cooperation with Cole, moved back the monkey's island with its compass and extended it to the width of the bridge to permit an unencumbered forward end; raised the front to about 6' 6", gave it a full-width platform, a windscreen *and* a slanting roof offering unprecedented protection from the elements. Old-timers condemned it as effete and obstructive to visibility. But it was the end of spray in the face of the men conning and commanding a destroyer.

Captain Lord Louis Mountbatten's *Kelly*, named after Sir John Kelly, captain of one of 'the big cats' in the First World War and later an Admiral of the Fleet, was to be the leader of the eight destroyers of the Fifth Flotilla, ready in the nick of time for this new war. The *Kelly*, with the black flotilla leader band round her funnel and finished immaculately in pale grey for Mediterranean service, ran her trials in July 1939. On the measured mile she made rather over 34 knots on 40,000 horsepower – no spectacular speed but all that she was designed to do, and her acceleration could throw you to the deck if you were not holding on. She was sweetly graceful, her appearance combining fine balance with purposeful aggression. Her Achilles' heel was inadequate protection against air attack.

The belief in the Royal Navy that future naval wars would be conducted between opposing battle fleets, with the naval air arm contributing useful reconnaissance and even effective bomb and torpedo attack against lighter vessels when conditions permitted, was slow to die, and in some circles was not dead until halfway through the war. The previous Tribal class had been designed on the principle that their anti-aircraft armament was primarily for the defence of the fleet, and not for self-defence, and that 'long range A. A. fire could be met if all the 4.7-inch guns could fire up to 40° elevation'. That is to say, if bombers flew overhead the destroyer was helpless to defend the fleet *or* itself. That 40° was defined as 'high angle' was a typical pre-Second World War compromise which lost the British many lives and many ships. Japanese destroyers had fully dual-purpose 5.1-inch guns (in gas-proof turrets at that) ten years earlier.

The *Kelly*'s light anti-aircraft armament was also inadequate. Apart from a single four-barrel 2-pounder pompom, a splendid weapon, there were only .5-inch and .303-inch machine-guns. During his recent period of service at the Naval Air Division Mountbatten had discovered how comparatively ineffectual solid-nosed bullets were against bombers with pilot's cabin and engines armour-plated (something RAF pilots learned in the Battle of Britain) and recognized that the most urgent requirement was for the smallest calibre, fastest-firing explosive shell gun, which made a nonsense of self-sealing fuel tanks and armour alike. He was among those who for long pressed for their adoption.

Finally, Mountbatten by-passed all authorities and went straight to the First Sea Lord, Sir Roger Backhouse, under whom he had served in the *Lion* in 1916, and personally persuaded him to over-rule the Admiralty hierarchy. The order for 20-mm Oerlikon cannons was placed too late for ships to mount them in the earliest days of the war, but the mounting was not difficult to fit and the *Kelly* got hers in 1941, along with the rest of the 5th Flotilla, before going to the Mediterranean.

The *Kelly* was different from the rest of the 5th Flotilla in one respect. Early in 1939 it had been arranged that the Royal Family on their forthcoming visit to Belgium should travel in the King's cousin's new ship, and she was accordingly equipped with the most luxurious quarters. It was intended that this should be a day trip, run at 30 knots both ways, a very comfortable speed for the destroyer. The war put paid to that exercise. Instead one of the *Kelly*'s early tasks was to bring her captain's cousin and the King's elder brother, the Duke of Windsor, and the Duchess, from France. The guests dined in the after cabins and later the Duke came up to the bridge on the cross-Channel journey.

By this time the *Kelly*'s light grey paintwork had been covered with stark dark grey, and instead of peacetime service in the warmth of the Mediterranean the flotilla leader had begun her arduous wartime duties in northern waters. Her life was destined to be brief, violent and highly eventful, to such a degree that her flotilla was soon to acquire the name 'The Fighting Fifth', and those appointed to it were told they 'would catch a packet all right' and that 'Lord Mountbatten, he's a proper death-or-glory boy!'

Admiral of the Fleet Sir James Somerville put it equally succinctly. At a press conference in Washington in 1944 when asked what he thought about the ex-captain of the *Kelly* and now Supreme Allied Commander in South-East Asia, he suggested that 'there is no one I would sooner be with in a tight corner, and no one who would get me into one sooner.'

Mountbatten had chosen the motto 'Keep On' for his ship because, above all, that was a destroyer's duty and one that was not always easy to honour in the teeth of a gale off Iceland. But Keep On she did, until the very end.

Within a few days of the outbreak of hostilities the *Kelly* heavily depth-charged a U-boat and – from the oil that arose from the depths – was awarded a 'probable' kill. Operating on convoy work out of Plymouth she got another U-boat for sure this time, and the submarine was seen to heave out of the water, helplessly crippled, and sink back again at an unnatural angle into its own oil. Whether in the Atlantic or Channel or the North Sea during those early months, the *Kelly* always seemed to be where there was most activity. When the aircraft carrier *Courageous* was sunk the *Kelly* raced through the night to the source of the SOS and picked up survivors, among them appropriately the ship's commander and lately an equerry to the King.

There was escort work as far north as Greenland that winter when the big ships were out looking for commerce-raiding heavy ships, and in those latitudes and in those seas the Mountbatten bridge proved its worth. The *Kelly* suffered her first serious damage, and her first tow home, just before Christmas 1939 – a time when the world thought the war was 'phoney' and the Royal Navy knew better.

The *Kelly* struck a mine. But no one could accuse her of being an unlucky ship after this episode, for the mine actually struck her several times, running most of the length of her keel before finally exploding clear of the ship's stern, wrenching her hull out of line and mauling her propellers. No one was injured but the destroyer lay helpless on the water, and it was another ship that brought her back to the Tyne for repairs. She was at sea again in February, was involved in the Norwegian campaign and experienced the fury of enemy dive-bomber attack for the first time. Off Namsos close by her a British and French destroyer were sunk and the *Kelly*'s light anti-aircraft gunners scored their first kill.

A few weeks later, in company with a cruiser and other destroyers, the *Kelly* was operating farther south in search of an enemy force consisting of a minelayer and a number of fast E-boats, the new German torpedo boats of the Second World War. On the evening of 9 May, in poor visibility, the *Kelly* was torpedoed at very close range. Mount-batten spotted the E-boat from the bridge, wrongly identified it as the conning tower of a U-boat, saw the torpedo's track. Then nothing. 'Thank God that was a dud!' the captain was heard to remark. A few seconds later there was an enormous explosion amidships. The *Kelly* had taken a torpedo in the forward boiler room, and Lord Mountbatten now believes that it was a second torpedo that got her. It made a colossal hole in the side of the boiler room.

The *Kelly* was doing 28 knots. She lay over heavily to starboard and at length came to rest amidst a cloud of steam and smoke. Many lay dead and dying. There was immediate flooding in one boiler room and the second was taking in water fast. Surely, it seemed, nothing could save her.

Damage control procedure had for long been a neglected activity in the Royal Navy. Shadows of the old Victorian tradition that preparing for the worst was defeatist and the arrogant assumption that British ships did not sink, still influenced Naval Staff priorities before the Second World War. When the *Kelly*'s captain had visited Pensacola in 1938 Admiral William 'Bull' Halsey had shown him how closely the United States Navy studied damage control. Mountbatten had passed on the lessons of American practice when he returned and applied them strongly to his own flotilla.

Remedial steps were taken fast on the *Kelly* as the destroyer heeled ever more steeply to starboard until the gunwale was awash. While repair parties went below to shore up the bulkheads the damage routine was followed on deck, all the ten torpedoes being fired set safe, the depth charges thrown overboard along with all the ready-use ammunition (the only mistake) and the boats, except for the whaler which was cast off for towing.

No one in the other ships present gave her long before she would go down, including Mountbatten's young nephew the Marquis of Milford Haven, Officer of the Watch in the *Kandahar*, *Kelly*'s next astern, who had seen the explosion and thought his uncle and his ship were done for. Only Mountbatten himself had confidence in the strength and durability of his ship. They were going to Keep On.

In the dark and with a heavy sea running the *Kelly* took in a tow line from the destroyer *Bulldog*, which lived up to her name as she gamely struggled with her awkward burden on a westerly course towards England. A few hours later a curious and fateful thing happened which the superstitious might ascribe to the hand of just retribution. A German E-boat – the same E-boat? – tore out of the darkness, collided with the *Bulldog*, bounced off, ran down the length of the *Kelly* shedding pieces[6] on the way and fell astern. Nothing more was seen, and all that was heard were the plaintive cries of her crew.

It took 91 hours to get the *Kelly* home, and few of them were uneventful. The tow repeatedly parted, a tug took over from the *Bulldog*, German bombers attacked them repeatedly and ammunition had to be brought up again from below, and the guns worked, entirely by hand. The dead were buried, the wounded tended and transferred.

In spite of a loss of 38 tons of topweight the *Kelly* continued to sink lower in the water. Mountbatten knew that the metacentric height, which governs the balance of a ship, was falling and that when it reached a negative point the ship would go over. Already the roll had a sinister sluggish quality about it. There was nothing more left to shed. Except men. And this the *Kelly* proceeded to do, transferring ten tons of sailor to the escorting ships, keeping himself and a small party of volunteers only onboard. Later he was told by Cole that this probably saved the ship from capsizing.

As the brave *Kelly* was dragged slowly up the Tyne the banks of the river, the cranes and piers of the dockyards and shipyards were thick with people cheering home their own ship. Later they put up in Hebburn churchyard a tablet in honour of the 27 dead, many of whom could only now be removed from the twisted wreckage of the ship.

It was not until December 1940 that the *Kelly* could put to sea again. Mountbatten, who meanwhile had been at sea with other Fifth Flotilla ships, took up command again of the repaired destroyer. Other officers were new. Among these was the First Lieutenant. His name was Lord Hugh Beresford. He was the great-nephew of Lord Charles Beresford, a brilliant but highly controversial naval figure before the First World War who had conceived a near-insane jealousy of Mountbatten's father and had heavily contributed to the hysteria which had brought about his resignation in 1914. Lord Hugh was a very different man, deeply religious, able, fearless and much loved by all, especially by his commander.

The *Kelly* was in the thick of it even before she had had time to work up, on escort and anti-U-boat work again, escorting minelayers off the French coast, answering shore battery fire, fighting off dive-bombers. Before long she was in dock again, damaged this time by exceptionally fierce seas. As events warmed up in the Mediterranean the 'Fighting Fifth' headed south for Gibraltar, then

Malta where they witnessed more intense bombing than they had ever seen. From this beleagured island they operated against Axis convoys to North Africa and bombarded German shore positions. German intervention in a campaign which had become an Italian fiasco was proving highly damaging to the British cause. When the Germans used paratroops to invade Crete on 20 May 1941 Mountbatten was ordered to lead his flotilla to the island to help destroy the German reinforcement and supply convoys from the mainland.

History now recognizes that the Crete campaign was one of the most ferocious of the war. The Royal Navy, without air cover and with inadequate anti-aircraft protection, suffered dreadful losses in cruisers and destroyers, and even the battleships present were badly damaged. But in reply they committed great execution and thousands of crack German troops were drowned.

Even before they reached the approaches to the island the *Kelly* was in action, scoring another 'probable' kill of a U-boat. During the first night off the island they sank several caiques packed with German reinforcement troops and fuel. Just before dawn on 23 May they were off the

German-held airfield of Maleme, bombarding it effectively. At daylight they headed south for Alexandria to refuel and re-ammunition. Mountbatten guessed they were in for a dangerous passage. He was right. German control of the air was total, their bomber force seemingly limitless in numbers, and ruthless and skilful in attack. Time and again the *Kelly*, by fast steaming and hard steering, dodged the bombs from high-level Junkers and Dorniers.

At 8 am on this beautiful clear morning Mountbatten was on the bridge reading his favourite Hornblower book *Ship of the Line* when the lookout sighted more trouble. This time it was 24 Stuka dive-bombers, seen against the rising sun. He pressed the alarm rattlers for full action stations, and the destroyer was made ready for her ordeal.

'The first party', wrote Mountbatten later,

> made for the *Kashmir*, and they started diving in waves of three. I could see the bombs dropping round her and all her guns were firing. Then a wave of three peeled off from our lot and started to dive. I put the telegraphs to 'full ahead'. I gave the order 'hard-a-starboard' to

bring the ship under the dive bomber to force it to dive ever steeper in the hopes they would finally be pushed beyond the vertical and lose control. This happened and the bomber hit the sea close by, sending up an enormous splash. I reversed the wheel 'hard-a-port'. The next dive bomber was also forced to dive steeper and steeper and this one we actually shot down into the sea. The next one also missed.

The *Kelly* could not keep up this brilliant evasion for ever. The *Kashmir* had already gone down. There were just too many Stukas in the sky, and one of them, coming down very low, its heavily canted wings and fixed undercarriage making it appear like a giant bird of prey plunging to the kill, dropped its 1,100-pound bomb smack onto the after gundeck, killing the guns' crew and many more below decks.

The *Kelly* was in a full starboard evasive turn. She never came out of it. When Mountbatten ordered the helm midships then hard-a-port, there was no response, nor any reply from the engine room. The end came with a terrible suddenness. The turn had caused the ship to heel over by about 20 degrees. The angle implacably increased with the speed of the water pouring in through the little ship's shattered stern.

At 30 knots the *Kelly* began to roll over, washing the crews from the guns they were still firing, and everyone else on deck, except her captain who was determined to follow tradition as far as it was physically possible and be the last to leave his ship. He only parted company with his bridge when it was upside down and he was on the point of drowning. As he and his navigator broke surface a cheery stoker petty officer remarked to them, 'Funny how the scum always comes to the top on these occasions.' All three 'scum' eventually reached the only raft which there had been time to release before the ship went over.

The raft was packed with men, many of them in a bad way. The Stukas had not finished with them, though. Down they came again, skimming the water and machine-gunning and killing the men who had thought their ordeal was nearly over. Again and again they came back while Mount-batten ordered the bodies of those who were killed to be gently dropped into the water to make room for the injured who were clinging on.

The *Kelly* was still afloat, upside down and almost awash, a buoyant credit to her toughness and the cunning that had gone into her construction, when the Stukas at last temporarily made off for more fuel and ammunition. Mountbatten organized some singing to keep up spirits, and when the destroyer made her last plunge he called for three cheers. But the voices were weak and husky from weariness and the oil that stung in their throats.

The lightly damaged *Kipling* succeeded in picking up most of the survivors. Later they picked up survivors on five rafts from the *Kashmir*. The ordeal by bomb and machine-gun was almost continuous. It ceased only shortly before they reached Alexandria. It was a packed ship, full of pain and anguish, that steamed slowly through the boom defences of the harbour and was welcomed by the sound of sirens and the cheers of ships' companies who knew what they had endured.

One hundred and thirty of the *Kelly*'s officers and men had gone down on that warm sunny morning in the Kithera Channel off Crete, more than half her company, including Beresford, for whom Mountbatten especially grieved. They are remembered with a plaque added to the headstone in the graveyard at Hebburn where lie the bodies of others who lost their lives in the fighting *Kelly*.

At the end of his speech of farewell to his remaining officers and men, in which he said that for the first time he felt unable to crack a joke with them, he told them that they would now be dispersed to replace men killed in other ships. 'The next time you are in action', he concluded, 'remember the *Kelly*. As you ram each shell home into the gun, shout "*Kelly!*" and so her spirit will go on inspiring us until victory is won.'

Bismarck

Battleship, 1941, Germany

The tradition of sturdiness laid down by von Tirpitz at the end of the nineteenth century was sustained during the rebuilding of the German navy in the 1930s. As before, designers were not content only with thick armour plate for protection. Elaborate and extensive compartmentation of the hull in this new generation of fighting ships ensured the localization of damage to the greatest possible extent. The emphasis on protective measures against torpedoes and aerial bombs acknowledged the power of the new twentieth-century weapons of sea warfare. In addition, a farsighted policy instituted before the Nazi government came into power in 1933, resulted in a close similarity in appearance between all German heavy units, which frequently confused the enemy, and sometimes themselves.

Their profile was low, sleek, purposeful, masculine and completely Teutonic, as if the designer of Mercedes cars had turned to marine architecture.

From the Phoenix ashes of the Kaiser's navy there emerged the new *Kriegsmarine*, its construction increasing in weight and pace with the growing iminence of another war. The Versailles Treaty had placed a limit of 10,000 tons on any German armoured ship, and the German navy under Admiral Hans Zenker, lately captain of the *Von der Tann*, was forced at least nominally to work within this severe restriction when the re-formation of a navy was first discussed in the early 1920s. After much debate and political conflict it was decided to build a compromise battleship-cruiser carrying an armament that would ensure the destruction of any cruiser opponent and with a speed to outpace any battleship.

The result of this thinking was the 'pocket battleship' *Deutschland* and her near-sisters *Admiral Scheer* and *Admiral von Spee*, built between 1928 and 1936. They possessed the same speed and broadside of 6 x 11-inch guns as the *Von der Tann* but possessed a much greater operating range and all on little more than half the displacement of that first battle cruiser. Much of the saving of weight was achieved by the use of a welded instead of a riveted hull, and diesel instead of steam turbine power. In fact the engines gave a lot of trouble throughout their lives, a severe drawback to vessels destined during their careers to engage in long-distance commerce raiding.

With the laying down by France of new fast battleships, the advent of Hitler, and the signature of the 1935 Naval Treaty with Britain, subsequent German heavy ship construction was bound to increase in size. The battle cruisers *Scharnhorst* and *Gneisenau* began, in 1936, as 26,000-tonners with 9 x 11-inch main armament and a speed of over 30 knots, but had grown by a further 6,000 tons on completion. They proved a thorn in the flesh of the British Admiralty for much of the Second World War. But, like the pocket battleships, they caused little damage to British shipping, and when the battleship *Duke of York* met the *Scharnhorst* in Arctic waters she had little trouble in sending her to the bottom with gunfire, backed up by destroyers' torpedoes.

Adolf Hitler had few of Kaiser Wilhelm's emotional sentiments towards sea power. His views upon naval rearmament wavered between enthusiasm and doubt. Admiral Erich Raeder, as the new head of the German navy, enjoyed a limited influence over the dictator by contrast with Field Marshal Hermann Goering, the head of the air force. *Luftwaffe* success and *Kriegsmarine* losses early in the war confirmed Hitler's doubts, and before long he had ordered the cancellation of orders for further battleships and even a carrier.

But if Hitler was a land animal under the strong influence of an air power fanatic, he also took pride in the revived *Kriegsmarine* and was prepared to approve a programme of naval construction, including U-boats, which might destroy Britain's commerce, something the Kaiser's navy had so nearly accomplished in 1917.

The *Bismarck* and *Tirpitz*, the apotheosis of German naval construction and two of the most powerful battleships ever built, were laid down in 1936, the *Bismarck* at the same Blöhm and Voss yard which had built the *Von der Tann*. In the full heat of Germany's patriotic and militaristic renaissance, the pace of construction was rapid, some 10,000 men working on the vessels in two shifts, so that they were ready for launching in early 1939. Hitler himself, with Raeder and Goering at his side, and the rest of the Nazi hierarchy present, gave the naming speech, announcing in the hectoring tones that had then become familiar to the whole world that she represented the resurrection of the German fleet, and that was something they regarded 'with particular love and sympathy'.

The *Bismarck*'s savage demeanour bore out her statistical summary of offensive and defensive attributes. There were bigger guns afloat than her 9 x 15-inch barrels but none more lethal than this new three-rounds-a-minute 38 cm weapon. German gunnery control had always been first class; its operation was now computerized and supported by radar. Of her 45,000 tons more than 38 per cent was devoted to armour protection, and her armament including the formidable secondary and anti-aircraft guns accounted for a further 7,500 tons. Yet this superbly designed man o'war could build up to a speed of 30 knots: a tough adversary indeed, as she was to prove herself to be.

—

When the *Bismarck* went to sea for the first time in August 1940, under the command of Captain

Ernst Lindemann, the German navy could boast a number of successes over the previous nine months, including the sinking of two British aircraft carriers, the battleship *Royal Oak*, cruisers and numerous destroyers. But German losses in the Norwegian campaign in particular had been heavy, and the new tonnage now joining the *Kriegsmarine* was badly needed.

The *Bismarck*'s first months were devoted to exhaustive trials and exercises with her complex equipment, much of it novel. Many of the exercises were carried out in company with the new heavy cruiser *Prinz Eugen*, with which it was intended that the battleship should operate on Atlantic sorties against Allied convoys, for which an elaborate support structure of supply and reconnaissance vessels was being set up. There could be no doubt that these two ships, working in unison with the *Gneisenau* and *Scharnhorst* from Brest on the French Atlantic seaboard, might have committed devastating damage in the crowded sea lanes and Western Approaches.

The Royal Navy, too, was commissioning new battleships as formidable as the *Bismarck*, but from long experience as a maritime power, the British knew the problems of successfully hunting down ocean raiders: you needed skill, intuition, luck and the application of superior power at a number of points on the wide ocean simultaneously. The raider always had the benefit of initiative and possessed other great advantages including surprise. But in this new age of air reconnaissance and radar, even in the Atlantic the *Bismarck* could not hope to remain for long undetected, and even the slightest damage from a lucky shot could fatally slow her down and make her the prey of weaker but more numerous forces.

Even before the planned date of the German naval sortie, Britain had some success with the newest weapons of sea warfare. The *Prinz Eugen* was damaged by a magnetic mine, the *Gneisenau* by RAF bombs and a suicidally delivered torpedo. But the *Bismarck* and the repaired *Prinz Eugen* got away at last on code-named operation 'Rheinübung' on 18 May 1941, just a few days before the *Kelly* embarked on her own last fatal mission. The overall commander was Admiral Gunther Lütjens flying his flag in the *Bismarck*. The departure signalled the start of a desperate double hunt, the Germans for fat, helpless convoys, the British for the predators.

During the following nine critical days every weapon of search, destruction and deceit was to be employed in the greatest pursuit and counterpursuit since the days of Villeneuve and Nelson 135 years earlier.

At the outset, nippy Intelligence on the British side weighted the advantages against Lütjens. But it was partly the Admiral's own fault for steaming through the narrow waters of the Kattegat and Skaggerak in broad daylight and unnecessarily close to the Scandinavian shore where agents worked for the Allied cause. Their passage was at once reported by the naval attaché in Stockholm and by concealed radio in Norway, and was passed urgently to Admiral John Tovey, C.-in-C. British Home Fleet at Scapa Flow in the Orkney Islands.

A day later, on 21 May. a specially equipped, reconnaissance, high-level Spitfire photographed two warships in Bergen harbour. The Germans never even saw the Spitfire in its blue-underwing camouflage at 25,000 feet, and it was screaming for home and beyond interception before radar picked it up. For Lütjens to lie in daylight at the Norwegian port closest to Britain was almost like trailing his coat. The next day another reconnaissance over

Bergen, this time at ultra low level, revealed that the Germans had left.

During the brief stay at Bergen the *Prinz Eugen* had oiled from a tanker. The *Bismarck* failed to do so for reasons no one has explained. Both ships painted out their jazzy camouflage with Royal Navy drab grey to confuse the enemy before heading north.

The luck swung towards Lütjens when the weather clamped down on these northern waters, and he steamed on unseen with the *Prinz Eugen*. But again faulty Intelligence let him down, and this time it was not his fault. German air reconnaissance of Scapa Flow appeared to reveal three capital ships, deluding the Admiral that the main units of the British fleet were still in their base. Two of the 'ships' were wooden dummies.

Lütjens continued thankfully on his long northward and circuitous course towards the Atlantic shipping lanes, encouraged by further false information that another powerful British group, Force H at Gibraltar, was heading deep into the Mediterranean with its carrier *Ark Royal*. It was doing no such thing. The weather remained in favour of the Germans for the most difficult and dangerous part of their voyage, between the Greenland ice pack and the British minefield lying less than 40 miles to the south, a passage narrow enough to cause navigation anxieties among the drifting ice floes, but not to cause the Admiral to reduce speed from his thundering 27 knots. Lütjens was like a driver who crosses an intersection flat out to reduce the chances of a collision.

Like Jervis, Collingwood or Nelson patrolling interminably off the French and Spanish ports 140 years earlier, the commanders of the patrolling British cruisers – Alfred 'Jerry' Phillips of the *Norfolk*, Robert Ellis of the *Suffolk* and many others – were weary of the weather and the tedium. But they and their men remained as alert as their forbears. They had radar. But it was a visual sighting by an AB on the bridge of the *Suffolk* which brought the long pursuit to a temporary conclusion. The *Bismarck*, vast and dark between mist patches to starboard, was momentarily observed at a terrifyingly short range. And then came the *Prinz Eugen*, almost as loomingly large it seemed to this sailor as he shouted, 'Two ships bearing Green One Four Oh!'

The Germans, over-dependent on their radar, were as surprised as their British hunters. The

Bismarck succeeded in straddling the *Suffolk's* consort *Norfolk* with some rapidly aimed salvos, but also knocked out her own primitive radar with the blast. Then they lost sight of the British ships in the cloud and fog, though they knew that they were being followed and that their position and course would now be broadcast to the whole Royal Navy.

Lütjens did not know of Hitler's warning words when Raeder had told him of the operation after the German ships were far out to sea: 'I want them recalled. Think what one aerial torpedo could do!' (Raeder had reassured him that the most dangerous part of the break-out had been successfully accomplished, and the Führer had then relented.)

The nearest British heavy units were only 300 miles distant. They were the battle cruiser *Hood* and the battleship *Prince of Wales*. On paper they should have been able to cope with the *Bismarck* and *Prinz Eugen* without too much difficulty: a combined broadside of 8 x 15-inch and 10 x 14-inch guns against the Bismarck's 9 x 15-inch and the cruiser's comparatively puny 8 x 8-inch. Their speed was about the same too. But the British battleship was too new, her crew not yet worked up. Trouble with her turrets and engines had not yet been sorted out and shipyard personnel were still onboard. The *Hood* was a mighty veteran, the only ship to slip through the Washington Treaty limitations. She was thin-skinned like all British battle cruisers dating back to an earlier war, a war in which three of her kind had been blown up by German guns within a couple of hours of combat.

These two big ships and their accompanying destroyers were under the command of Vice-Admiral Lancelot Holland who flew his flag in the *Hood*. He was a gunnery specialist, the very man for the task, you would think. At 8.04 pm on 23 May he learned of the course and position of the *Bismarck*, altered his own course to 295 degrees and speed up to 27 knots. 'Action can be expected within a few hours', was broadcast over the ships' loud-speakers. Tomorrow was Empire Day, a splendid day for battle and victory.

Through the long Arctic evening and into the snow-flurried night the *Bismarck* stormed south-west, her 150,000-horsepower turbines sweeping her through the water now at her maximum 30 knots, and consuming her already depleted oil supplies at a vast rate. Lütjens was worried on two counts. He could not throw off the two, shadowing, old cruisers, and it was evident from the signals they were making (and his cryptographers were decoding them as fast as they were transmitted) that not only had the British got radar, but that it was highly efficient by contrast with his own – which was unserviceable anyway.

With the breaking of the Arctic dawn Captain Leach of the *Prince of Wales* ordered a boy from the bridge to go high up into the crow's nest with an extra duffel coat and an extra powerful pair of binoculars. It was as if radio and sound detectors and radar had never been invented; and when the boy yelled down 'Enemy in sight!' it might have been his forbear spotting the combined fleet emerging from Cadiz before Trafalgar.

The appearance of the two British ships 20 miles to the east came as a complete surprise to Lutjens. At first they were misidentified as cruisers, but when the word reached him that the leading British ship was the *Hood*, as big and heavily armed as the *Bismarck*, and the other a modern battleship, he knew that he could not avoid combat and that the odds were against him.

The *Bismarck* opened fire on the *Hood* at 5.53 am. It might have been Coronel in 1914 when poor 'Kit'

Cradock met the crack German gunnery armoured cruisers off Chile. The *Bismarck*'s and *Prinz Eugen*'s shooting was sublime. With an early salvo they made a hit, causing a fire to break out. A minute later, 6.01 precisely, a plunging 15-inch shell struck the *Hood* amidships, penetrated deep down into the ship's magazine and exploded. The result was equal to a simultaneous hit by hundreds of 15-inch shells. The 42,000-ton battle cruiser was torn in two, the flash of flame reaching hundreds of feet into the sky. The bows stood upright for a moment, like a giant speedboat gone berserk. Then there was just falling wreckage and a boiling cauldron of Arctic Ocean. The gunnery specialist admiral, the captain, every officer – more than 1,400 in all went down in the remains of their ship. Two seamen and a midshipman were later found, miraculously alive.

Then it was the *Prince of Wales*'s turn. Already the elevating gear of one of her 14-inch guns had failed and the aft four-gun turret had not been able to fire because at first the ships had approached the enemy on too fine a bearing. The civilian workmen onboard the battleship were there to check gun faults not fight battles with them. Willy-nilly they were now doing both. In spite of their efforts one after another of the new ship's guns broke down, and Leach was forced to break off the action and join the cruisers.

One sunk, the other running. Amongst most of those in the *Bismarck* and *Prinz Eugen* there was jubilation. All-powerful, invincible *Bismarck*!

Lütjens and the shrewder members of his staff did not see the situation as simply as that. Splendid gunnery had sent to the bottom the old *Hood*, biggest warship in the world for 20 years, and damaged the Royal Navy's most modern battle-ship. But the *Bismarck* had not come out of the contest unscathed. Three 14-inch shells had struck her. One had damaged a boiler room, reducing the ship's speed marginally. Another which had not even exploded – shades of Jutland! – had penetrated two oil tanks, depriving the engines of 1,000 tons of precious oil, while more, mixed with incoming seawater, spilled out, leaving a tell-tale trail like the blood of a hunted animal. She was listing nine degrees to port and was three degrees down at her bows.

Studied with the benefit of hindsight, the German success had a parallel in the Japanese victory at Pearl Harbor six months later. By simple statistical calculation temporary victory must now turn to eventual and permanent defeat. For the loss of the *Bismarck* would spell the end of German surface raiding on any scale. The loss of the *Hood* was to the British a loss of some $7\frac{1}{2}$ per cent of capital ship strength. To the Germans the loss of the *Bismarck* was the loss of 50 per cent of her battleship strength.

Lütjens decided to call off the sortie and endeavour to reach the nearest port without delay. He detached the undamaged *Prinz Eugen*, which got back safely on 1 June, and headed for the French coast, hoping on the way to throw off her tenacious pursuers, the *Suffolk* and *Norfolk*. He succeeded in doing just this, and in casting the British Admiralty in London into a state of considerable alarm. Destroyers, cruisers, aircraft carriers, battleships and battle cruisers along with aircraft of Coastal Command, were brought urgently into the search, convoys and submarines alerted. Churchill appealed to the neutral USA for help in finding the *Bismarck* – '…Give us the news and we will finish the job.'

For $31\frac{1}{2}$ hours the *Bismarck* remained undetected while she steamed south-east between the 50th and

60th parallels towards safety. Now it was the turn of air power to play the dominant and crucial role. On the morning of 26 May, a hazy, cloudy morning with a heavy sea, the *Bismarck*'s lookouts spotted a large, clumsy-looking twin-engined machine flying straight at the battleship at a mere 500 feet. The anti-aircraft gunners at once opened fire on this juicy target, but the aircraft, now identified as a flying boat, disappeared into a cloud. A minute later she was seen again, now at 2,000 feet and right above.

Fire was opened again with renewed urgency by some 100 guns of many calibres in an effort to blow up this intruder before she could get off a radio message. The flying boat took laboured, evasive action in the few seconds she was in the sights of the *Bismarck*'s gunners and hits were scored, they were sure. But the flash of flame that would mark her end was never seen, and almost at once the battleship's cryptographers were decoding the signal from the plane announcing simultaneously to the two warring navies, and the whole world, the position of the hunted vessel:

One battleship bearing 240° 5 miles,
course 150°, my position 49° 33' north,
21° 47' west. Time of origin 1030/26.

Churchill's appeal to Roosevelt had been answered in full measure. The flying boat was one of a number of American Consolidated PBYs, named Catalinas by the RAF, which had recently been lend-leased to Britain, the product of an earlier appeal from the British prime minister, 'Give us the tools and we'll finish the job.' With the Catalinas came a number of American airmen carrying the time-honoured euphemistic title of 'special observer' to instruct the British in the handling of the flying boats. The co-pilot of the Catalina which had sighted the *Bismarck* was Ensign Leonard 'Tuck' Smith USN, aged 26 years, from Higginsville, Missouri, experienced in flying the Catalina, inexperienced in combat operations.

It was a perfect Anglo-American sortie which was to have profound consequences on the Battle of the Atlantic months before America became a combatant.

Among all the calculations that were speedily made the one that stood out in its undeniable accuracy was simple: the *Bismarck* must be inter-cepted and destroyed within 24 hours. After that the battleship might be safe under the steel umbrella of countless German land-based bombers.

The next blow to the Germans – a physical one this time – again came from the air. The carrier *Ark Royal*, according to German Intelligence still in the Mediterranean, was instead hastening from the sunshine and now, with her range of fire limited only by the endurance of her aircraft, was most favoured for making the next attack. It began with a mishap, potentially the most fateful of all the many experienced by hunter and hunted alike. She launched nine of her slow, biplane, Swordfish torpedo bombers without being warned in time of the presence close to their target of the cruiser *Sheffield*. In the excitement of imminent combat and in poor visibility the planes confused the *Sheffield* with the enemy and launched their 'tin fish' at her. Mercifully and skilfully, the cruiser combed them all. Recognizing their blunder, one of the Swordfish flashed contritely by lamp, 'Sorry for the kipper'.

The torpedo bombers quickly made amends for their error. Re-armed, they took off again and closed on the giant ship at 9 pm below cloud and in failing light. The *Bismarck*'s gunners saw them coming in on their brave, un-coordinated attack, wheels almost brushing the wavetops, one by one. This was not what the *Bismarck* feared. An earlier attack from another carrier had been brushed aside without difficulty, and the one hit that had been made had scarcely dented the ship's armour plate. Besides, how could these machines hope to survive the ferocity of the gunfire that tore out to meet them as they steadied for their launching run?

Some of the Swordfish were hit time and again, others flinched back from the barrage of tracer as it threatened to envelop them. Yet all incredibly survived and two scored hits. One exploded harmlessly against her tough hull. The second – the millionth chance blow the prescient Hitler had feared – struck her right aft, jamming her steering gear.

Slowly the *Bismarck* turned to port, continued to turn, heeling hard over, until the wind that had been tearing over her stern now buffeted head on at her bridge. Then she was heading south-west, south, back momentarily on her old course. Round she turned, her rudder fixed at 15 degrees, circling implacably as darkness closed about the ship, and Captain Lindemann ordered a reduction in speed.

It was a foul night with a gale blowing, the rain squalls indistinguishable from the spray that struck like shell fragments. The *Bismarck* lay wallowing in the darkness, a low sulky grey shape, crippled by a little old biplane that cost under £10,000, awaiting her fate. Lütjens signalled Berlin, 'Ship unmanoeuvrable. We fight to the last shell. Long live the Führer.' (The dictator was at the movies watching reassuring propaganda films.)

The *Bismarck*'s sting was no less lethal for her seized rudders. When destroyers tore at her from the black, hellish seas, she opened up with her radar-directed guns to such effect that one after another they were beaten back. Lütjens and his staff knew that they would be facing more formidable antagonists at dawn. And alone. Bombers could be of little help in these conditions and although all U-boats in the proximity had been ordered to her aid it was unlikely that any could make it before daylight.

At dawn the sea was empty. It was as if by some divine deliverance the Atlantic had been swept clear of the numerous enemy. The illusion was brief.

Reality was a cruiser coming up fast from the north-west. She was the *Norfolk*, the same heavy cruiser which had held them with such tenacity off Greenland all that time ago – could it really be only three days? She had witnessed the end of the *Hood*. Now she was at the ringside again in this awful game of giant tit-for-tat.

The battleships arrived as inevitably as the daylight itself. They emerged out of the haze and spume dead ahead, the *Rodney* and the *King George V. Rodney* alone out-gunned the *Bismarck*, and the enemy possessed the priceless power to manoeuvre, to evade the fall of shell, to choose the most favourable bearing.

Fire opened at 8.47 am with the support of the *Norfolk* and later the *Dorsetshire*. At first the German shooting was spirited, then it fell off badly as spirits were crushed like the structure of their own ship, and not one hit was secured. One by one the guns were put out of action and the hull of the great battleship was turned into a white-hot shambles of twisted steel, exploding ammunition and burst pipes. From the point-blank range at which the two British battleships ceased fire, men could be seen racing aft and hurling themselves into the sea to escape. 'What the ship was like inside did not bear thinking about,' remarked one shocked witness.

The *Bismarck* never surrendered. At 10.15 am the *Dorsetshire* launched torpedoes at her port and starboard sides in turn. At the same time survivors of the holocaust deep down in the ship laid explosive charges in the sea valves. So it was suicide in the end. At no point had her side armour been pierced, and her engines were intact when she capsized and went down. She was, as her makers had claimed, as near unsinkable as a battleship could be made.

The *Dorsetshire* and the destroyer *Maori* were deputed to pick up survivors. Rescue work was handicapped by the high seas and the inevitable oil slicks. No boats could be launched. One hundred and ten men were dragged by ropes out of the Atlantic. Many more could have been saved but for the tragic intervention of a suspected U-boat, which led to immediate orders to ring down for full speed.

The loss of the *Bismarck* was a stunning blow to the German nation and caused deep relief and thankfulness throughout Britain at a time when she was alone and good news was scarce.

The nine-day cruise of the *Bismarck* sounded stridently almost every note of drama in sea warfare and was characterized by more chances and narrow margins than any novelist would be permitted. There was brilliance and folly on both sides. If the *Bismarck* had refuelled at Bergen she could have steamed at full speed on that last critical day and perhaps made Brest. If Admiral Holland had positioned his ships so that all 18 instead of only ten of his heavy guns could bear on the enemy, and had ordered the *Suffolk* and *Norfolk* to his support, he might have saved the *Hood*. But great skills were exhibited too and the Royal Navy committed fewer errors than on that last occasion 25 years earlier when German and British battleships fought at Jutland.

The British had the better luck this time. Perhaps in the celestial counting house it was felt they deserved it after the French fiasco, Dunkirk and a winter of bombing. A year later, almost to the day, another PBY Catalina, this time captained by Lieutenant Howard Ady USN, spotted through scattered cloud Japanese carriers heading for Midway. The consequences of this piece of reconnaissance luck were to be as profound as

Ensign Smith's – the destruction of a carrier force that was the backbone of Japanese sea power. America needed the good news, too, in 1942.

New Jersey

Battleship, 1943, USA

Towards the end of 1967 I was invited to the US Naval Shipyard at Philadelphia to study the refitting of one of the navy's latest surviving battleships. I had agreed to write the script for a television film which was to be shown to the American people when the battleship was recommissioned and steamed off to Vietnam.

It was a most moving and exhilarating experience to witness the enthusiasm with which the navy was setting about the task of reactivating this great battleship, the *New Jersey*, for the second time since her retirement. Perhaps I imagined it, but I thought I discerned a fresh fire in the eyes of Pentagon admirals in Washington for whom the golden days of their service were spent in Pacific Fleet battleships in the 1940s.

A new supersonic fighter plane had proved a disappointment, I was told with some relish, so the defence chiefs had been obliged to consider the gunfire of the battleship as an alternative; for had not the 14-inch and 16-inch guns of the navy's battlewaggons proved their worth time and time again in bombardments in the war against Japan and later in Korea? Other mothballed battleships, I was told, were being considered for reactivation, too.

It was many years since I had set eyes on a battleship. At the naval shipyard there were three, all within a cable's length of each other. The *Iowa* and *Wisconsin* lay anchored side by side like two aged Navy Club admirals in adjacent chairs for comfort and reminiscence.

I went onboard the *Iowa*, lingered beneath her 16-inch rifles, climbed up her massive bridgework with the obsolete radar aerials which had once been the novelty of their day, passed my hand over a deep scar from an enemy shell. The only sounds were from wheeling gulls and squabbling pigeons who nested with complete security up here, and the perpetual but muted murmuring that you hear onboard any moored vessel.

Below decks there was the chill of the morgue, and only dim light from a sketchy electric circuit. On the mess decks, in the ward room, the sleeping quarters, it was as if the ship's company had given the *Iowa* a last spring clean, and quit in a body. The coffee cups were lined up just so, the bunks made up with fresh linen, the stainless steel tables wiped down and glinting dully. Only the captain's cabin had been forgotten by some wayward steward, the bed still rumpled from that last night in February 1958.

The last date of this battleship's active life was confirmed by the open copy of *Look* magazine on the deck and the now brown-edged notices, listing orders and names of sailors who might now be middle-aged civilians, on the notice board.

I had recently published a book in America under the title *Death of the Battleship*. Here was the reality. Yet the *Iowa*, like her sister, could soon have been put back into service...

The picket boat took me back to the pier and to the contrasting *New Jersey*, bustling with dockyard men working in shifts through the day and night to ready her for war again. They were fitting her out with new computers and radar to make the firing of her main batteries even more accurate, new electronics and electrical communications, new domestic equipment, air conditioning for these softer times, a helicopter deck aft, Zuni rocket launchers and fire-fighting system.

Ironically, 26 years after Pearl Harbor, which history has told us marked the final triumph of air power over the battleship, they were stripping the *New Jersey* of her 64 multi-barrel 40 mm anti-aircraft guns. She could manage without them. But this, I learned, was only on the comfortable assumption that the battleship would be covered by American fighters during her new tour of active duty.

I had fallen in love with the battleship at 12 years old. Like every first love affair, it can never be forgotten, and 33 years later here I was in a daze of renewed adoration, touching the reality, walking the decks, studying the guns. I would willingly have slung my hammock there and then and remained onboard until she put to sea. But my producer thought I must now have completed my research. A few weeks later the *New Jersey* steamed slowly down the Delaware, just as she had for the first time in May 1943, off to war again as the world's last active battleship.

Like the *Bismarck*, the *New Jersey* was one of the last generation of super-Dreadnoughts, the ultimate gun platform at a time when the gun was still a useful weapon but no longer the arbiter in sea warfare. Like Japan and Britain, the other two major naval powers in the 1930s, the United States turned to the battleship again with the growing imminence of war from 1935. A few months after Britain laid down her first battleship for 15 years, America laid down the *North Carolina* (BB 55) at New York Navy Yard in October 1937.

The skills required to create an organism as complex as a super-Dreadnought are highly specialized and the machinery and the men alike required to roll special, hardened, armour plate or rifle the barrel of 16-inch ordnance had become rusty. There had also been technological advances over the years which added to the complexity of introducing a substantial new programme of battleship construction.

The design of the North Carolina class was also inhibited by the last vestiges of conformity to international agreements, which had in fact been perfunctorily tossed aside by America's future foes, Japan and Germany. Displacement was therefore limited to 35,000 tons although rumours that Japan was building 16-inch-gunned ships (actually 18.1-inch) caused the Bureau of Construction, unlike its British counterpart, to shelve plans for 14-inch main armament.

The two North Carolinas, armed with 9 x 16-inch and able to steam 28 knots, were completed before hostilities with Japan commenced, and both were despatched to European waters to augment the British Home Fleet, as had happened in 1917. Their appearance was reminiscent of the last American class completed in 1923, although the lattice masts so favoured by the US Navy had been replaced by orthodox pole masts. The ships were admired by the Royal Navy and they did sterling service with the Russian-bound convoys before transferring to the Pacific.

The four ships of the next class were similar to the North Carolinas although greater emphasis than ever was laid on protection, the weight of which was compensated for by concentrating the machinery and thus reducing the overall length. A single funnel instead of twin, and a bunched-up effect amidships gave this class a decidedly Teutonic silhouette.

War was already raging in Europe when the *New Jersey* was laid down in September 1940 as one of a planned class of six battleships intended to form a fast wing to outpace any group of Japanese battleships or battle cruisers. In terms of strength they were the equal of the *Bismarck*, in gunpower and speed superior. How they would have fared in direct ship-to-ship combat with the last Japanese battleships will never be known. The *Yamato* and *Musashi*, the biggest battleships ever built, could no doubt have outranged them with their 18.1-inch guns, and the ability of even the superbly protected *New Jersey* to withstand a plunging salvo of these shells must be judged doubtful. On the other hand, with a speed superiority of at least eight knots the *New Jersey* would have governed the tactical movements of any engagement.

But regardless of the quality of these American ultimate battleships (and that was very high) the impossibility of Japan finally defeating the United States at sea was confirmed in theory and in the event by the great American superiority in industrial and manpower resources. While the Japanese struggled to complete their two monsters in four to four and a half years, utilizing a great proportion of their shipbuilding capacity, the Americans completed the *New Jersey* in 32 months and took the construction of the class of four in their stride (the last two were cancelled).

This battleship which was to fight in three of America's twentieth-century wars followed recent American practice of mounting 9 x 16-inch guns each capable of firing a 2,100-pound shell some 23 miles, in three turrets. In addition there were 20 x 5-inch dual-purpose secondary guns and massive batteries of light anti-aircraft guns.

There was a marked change in the protective capacity of the *New Jersey* by contrast with the earlier classes. Here, as I was able to see for myself, the emphasis was more on very thick and deep external armour plate rather than a complex framework of internal plate. Proper recognition of the increasing weight and penetration of bombs was seen in the horizontal protection, and although no hint of the ultra-destructive Long Lance oxygen-charged 24-inch torpedo had filtered through the Japanese security net, the *New Jersey* boasted superior underwater protection to any preceding American battleship.

The engine room is a giant storehouse of sheer power, a miracle of the art of marine engineering. In the *New Jersey* there are four Westinghouse geared turbines, eight Babcock and Wilcox boilers, driving four shafts to meet the designed output of 212,000 horsepower. She had no difficulty in making 35 knots on her trials and frequently hit this figure during her operational life.

–

After fighting 'in the line' from the Anglo-Dutch wars until Jutland, the coming of air power had forced the battleship to relinquish its primary role as final arbiter of naval power. Instead, the *New Jersey* and her consorts in the Pacific were to play twin subsidiary roles, as shore bombardment vessels and as escort and protector of the new capital ships, the carriers.

The *New Jersey* passed through the Panama Canal on 7 January 1944 to begin her first period of war service. Almost at once she was involved in the task of screening with her multitudinous light batteries the carrier task force whose planes were attacking Kwajalein and Eniwetok in the Marshall Islands.

With the successful invasion of these islands, the *New Jersey*, under the command of Captain Carl F. Holden, became the flagship of Admiral Raymond Spruance, a brilliant commander who had been largely responsible for the victory at Midway two years earlier.

The Japanese fortress island of Truk was the first target of Spruance's Fifth Fleet. In the ensuing combats the Task Force accounted for nine Japanese cruisers, auxiliary cruisers and destroyers as well as numerous other auxiliary craft – some 40 in all. In the following months the battleship was deeply engaged in support operations in which her heavy guns bombarded stores, troop concentrations, shipping, airfields and other targets, while her anti-aircraft batteries filled the sky with a screen of bullets and shells which proved virtually impenetrable.

At the tragic yet flippantly named 'Marianas Turkey Shoot' in the June battle of the Philippine Sea, the *New Jersey* took her share of the score of almost 400 downed Japanese planes, most crewed by raw beginners. The streaming tracers, the grey puffs, and the trails of smoke and flame together spelt out as if in skywriting the end of once-vaunted Japanese naval air power.

In August 1944 the *New Jersey* piped onboard her second distinguished admiral, 'Bull' Halsey, and the flagship took part in the controversial diversion in the Battle of Leyte Gulf in October. Halsey was tempted away from the centre of the struggle, leaving vulnerable forces with inadequate cover. The *New Jersey* sank no surface vessels, as she certainly would have done but for the recall, in the ferocious engagements of that widespread and prolonged battle. But planes from the carriers she protected sank a battleship and enemy carriers.

Time and again her exceptional speed was invaluable, and proved correct Admiral Fisher's priority scale when he ordered the world's fastest big ships between 1905 and 1915. The *New Jersey* could outpace any of the carriers she was deputed to cover, her combined grace and power matching the ideals of the British admiral who had been so proud of his 'ocean greyhounds'.

At the turn of the years 1944–5, with Japanese resistance beginning to crumble, the *New Jersey*'s 16-inch guns threw salvoes ashore at Okinawa and

Luzon, Formosa and Amoy, and numerous other shores. As an honourable climax to her wartime operations, she screened the carrier *Essex* as it closed on Tokyo, despatching her bombers at the capital city's aircraft factories. Later, after a refit and the surrender, she engaged on the happier task of bringing home servicemen.

With the end of the Second World War, it was a tamer, more ceremonial life for the battleship. There were training cruises to European waters, formal visits to Royal Navy ports, a reception for the King of Norway.

The *New Jersey*'s second war career began on 20 May 1951 when, flying the flag of Vice-Admiral Harold M. Martin, her big guns spoke again, bombarding Wonsan. Her first ever casualties occurred a few days later as a result of a North Korean shell hit. Over the following months the *New Jersey* acquired a high reputation for the accuracy of her shooting. It was said she could put a 16-inch shell on a mortar battery at any range she chose, and it was a stunning experience for enemy troops, many miles inland, to experience the impact of exploding shells falling from a clear sky. Bridges, concentrations of transports and trains, artillery batteries, trenches and bunkers, oil refineries and tunnels – all suffered from her 16-inch and 5-inch shells as the battleship ranged up and down the coast.

At the end of the year she was ordered home for a rest and refit. On her return to duty she celebrated and confirmed her old prowess by making seven hits with seven shells on a communications building. With the end of the Korean War the *New Jersey* again returned to European waters for a tour of duty with the Sixth Fleet in the Mediterranean and for a midshipmen's cruise. Many senior officers in the US Navy today first went to sea onboard the *New Jersey* in the years between 1947 and 1956 for training exercises. Then on 21 August 1957 the veteran was decommissioned and began her second long period mothballed in home waters.

A decade passed before the surprise decision was made to ready her for action again, against a new foe in new eastern waters. But this time she was alone, the only active battleship in the world. Nothing remained afloat of that once formidable Japanese battleship fleet. The British had scrapped their last battleship, the *Vanguard*, eight years earlier.

For six months the *New Jersey* conducted a series of bombardments against shore targets, many of which were inaccessible to aircraft or which could not be reached because of unfavourable weather. The *New Jersey* with her sophisticated equipment could fire in any weather, and her shooting was more accurate than ever before. In all she fired over 6,000 16-inch shells, as many as in the Korean War and almost ten times as many as in her first war career.

The battleship has often been defined as 'the supreme deterrent'. The *New Jersey*'s last hostile act was in this capacity. With her duties fulfilled the battleship was on her way home when on 15 April 1969 a North Korean plane shot down an American surveillance plane, killing the crew.

In the diplomatic crisis that ensued, a carrier task force prepared for the worst consequences, and the *New Jersey* was ordered to reverse course and provide it with the protection of its big guns. This did the trick. In this last act of what was once called Gunboat Diplomacy, the affair was settled amicably, and the battleship resumed the voyage that was to prove her last.

Or was it? She is still afloat today, and it is a comforting thought for all battleship lovers that her guns remain ready for action. In the ceremony of hauling down her colours her commanding officer made a brief speech. 'Rest well, yet sleep lightly', he adjured, 'and hear the call, if again sounded, to provide firepower for freedom.'

Some Terms Explained

Athwartships A direction across from one side of a ship to the other.

Backing (and filling) Bracing the yards so that the wind presses on the forward side of the sail. Filling is the reverse operation.

Bar socket The cavity in a capstan into which a bar is inserted for turning it. Also called pigeon hole.

Barbette The trunk of a gun mounting on which the turret revolves.

Beakhead The part of a sailing ship forward of the forecastle, and traditionally the seamen's lavatory. Thus 'heads' for lavatories in the Royal Navy today.

Belt (armour) The length of armour applied to the side of a warship.

Bowsprit A spar projecting over a vessel's bows.

Caravel Small Mediterranean trading vessel, later adopted and modified by the Spanish and Portuguese for voyages of exploration.

Carrack A larger version of the above.

Close-hauled Sailing as close to the wind as possible with sails full.

Culverin A long-barrelled, relatively small-calibre early naval gun with a long range. Demi–culverin fired a shot of about half the weight, 9 pounds.

Double To sail round.

Double-headed shot A gun loaded with twice its normal shot, but with consequent reduced range.

Draught (draft) The depth of water a ship draws, or occupies.

Fighting tops The masthead platform manned in battle by personnel with muskets.

Gage The advantageous windward side of an enemy occupied by his antagonist in sailing warfare.

Halyards Ropes used to hoist or lower sails.

Jib boom A continuation of the bowsprit.

Knee A right-angle bar to provide additional strength between a ship's timbers.

Lattice mast A mast made of numerous laced metal girders unique to American constructors *c.* 1890–1920.

Lee shore The coastline on which a wind blows, and thus a hazard to a sailing vessel.

Lid A cover for a ship's gun when not in use, usually hinged.

Mizzen The third mast of a sailing ship. Bonaventure mizzen: the fourth mast for a lateen (triangular) sail and rare after 18th century.

Pennant (pendant) Narrow tapering flag, mainly used for signalling or to designate a special purpose.

Rake Angle of overhang of bow or stern; also angle of masts and funnels.

Shrouds The rigging (ropes) of a sailing vessel providing lateral support for masts. (Stays provide fore and aft support.)

Spritsail Small square sail beneath the bowsprit.

Stand (for) Set course towards.

Step Framework to hold the base (heel) of a mast. Also verb.

Strike (colours) Lower the flag in surrender.

Taffrail The after rail at the stern of a ship.

'Teredo navalis' A dreaded boring mollusc, later countered by fitting copper sheathing to the bottom of sailing ships.

Topsail The second sail up, above the course, from the deck.

Tripod mast A form of three-legged mast in larger steel men o'war favoured by the British navy. cf. Lattice mast.

Tumblehome The angle at which the two sides of a ship's hull are brought in towards the centre line from the maximum beam, giving a tubby appearance.

Waist The upper deck between fore and main masts.

Warp Moving a ship by a hawser (warp) by manpower and usually with the aid of a capstan or small anchor.

Book List

Bennett, G. *Naval Battles of the First World War* (London, 1968)

Blok, P. J. *Michiel Adriaanszoon de Ruyter* (Gravenhage, 1928)

Breyer, S. *Battleships and Battle Cruisers 1905–1970* (London, 1973)

Chalmers, W. S. *David, Earl Beatty* (London, 1951)

Corbett, J. *Naval Operations 1914–18* (London, 1920)

Costello. J. and Hughes, T. *Jutland 1916* (London, 1976)

Grenfell. R. *The Bismarck Episode* (London, 1948)

Hough, R. *The Fleet That Had to Die* (London, 1958)

Hough, R. *The Hunting of Force Z* (London, 1963)

Kemp. P. (Ed.) *History of the Royal Navy* (London, 1969)

Kemp, P. (Ed.) *The Oxford Companion to Ships and the Sea* (London, 1976)

Kennedy, L. *Pursuit: the Chase and Sinking of the Battleship Bismarck* (New York, 1974)

Macintyre, D. *The Battle for the Pacific* (London, 1966)

Macintyre, D. *Jutland* (London, 1957)

Marsh, E. J. *British Destroyers* (London, 1966)

Miller, N. *Sea of Glory* (New York, 1974)

Morison, S. E. *John Paul Jones* (London, 1959)

Parkes, O. *British Battleships* (London, 1958)

Poolman, K. *The Kelly* (London, 1954)

Preston, A. (Ed.) *Warship Profiles*, vol. ii (London, 1973)

Roskill, S. *The War at Sea*, 3 vols. (London, 1954–6)

Roskill, S. *The Warspite* (London, 1957)

Smith, P. C. F. *The Frigate Essex Papers: Building the Salem Frigate 1798–9* (Salem. 1974)

A True Narrative of the Engagement between His Majesty's Fleet and that of Holland (London, 1666)

Vere, F. *Salt in Their Blood* (London, 1955)

Warner, O. *Great Battle Fleets* (London, 1973)

Notes

1. A system of rating, or classifying, fighting ships was introduced into most navies in the seventeenth century. In the Royal Navy the classification was: 1st rate, 100 guns; 2nd rate, 52 guns; 3rd rate, 46 guns; 4th rate, 40 guns; 5th rate, 24 guns; 6th rate, 18 guns.

2. The *Indefatigable* had been firing shells weighing 850 pounds. These were of 1,950 pounds.

3. During this naval war both sides courted disaster by putting pre-Dreadnought armoured ships against Dreadnoughts, almost always with fatal results – for the British and Germans at Jutland, for the Germans at the Battle of the Falkland Islands – and now here at the Dogger Bank.

4. The Dogger Bank engagement was the first naval battle in which air power played a part, albeit indirectly. The German battle cruiser *Von der Tann* was absent because in a bombing raid on Christmas Day she had weighed anchor in such haste that she had badly damaged herself in collision. The additional weight of her salvoes might well have resulted in the *Lion*'s destruction – she did, after all, single-handedly destroy the battle cruiser *Indefatigable* later. Then, many more of the *Blücher*'s crew could have been picked up if this mercy operation had not been abandoned when the British ships were bombed from the air.

5. Lord Mountbatten, reading this chapter in manuscript, pointed out that this ship was captured by the British in 1815 to become the fourth ship of this name. The 8th *President*, depot ship of the Royal Naval Reserve, lies alongside the Embankment in London today. It is on her books that Lord Mountbatten draws his pay today.

6. The steering wheel is today a trophy at Lord Mountbatten's home.